David Thompson

James K. Smith

CANADA

POSTES

5¢

POSTAGE

DAVID THOMPSON 1770 — 1857

Fitzhenry & Whiteside Limited

Contents

The Author

James K. Smith is a prominent author and editor of Canadian educational texts. He has a special interest and expertise in the history of Canadian explorers and the fur trade.

To the David Thompson

© *1975 Fitzhenry & Whiteside Limited*
150 Lesmill Road
Don Mills, Ontario, M3B 2T5

Printed and bound in Canada

ISBN-0-88902-215-5

Hudson Bay Chapter 1

He had a snub nose. His hair was dark, his skin
sallow. The boy was downright homely. Small and
chunky, dressed in dark, coarse, woollen jacket and
trousers, to the officers and men of the Hudson's Bay
Company's ship *Prince Rupert* he was not worth a
second glance: just another son from another penniless
family on his way to a job in North America with the
Company. Scores of such youngsters had been sent
out to the Bay before. There was nothing new in the
sight of a blank-faced boy, usually seasick-green,
gazing glumly out to sea. But although David
Thompson had his eyes fixed on the leaden waters of
Hudson Bay, he was neither queasy nor bored.

It was early in September, 1784. That year, the Bay
was so choked with ice that the *Prince Rupert* was still
moving very slowly southward almost a month after
entering the huge inland sea. In fact, out on the
Atlantic, as the ship approached the straits leading to
the Bay, for days on end hundreds of icebergs had
slowed the vessel's speed to little more than a crawl.
Yet David was still fascinated by the varying shapes
and colours of something as simple as frozen water.
No two icebergs looked the same. Different light
intensities played tricks with one's vision and turned
bergs into fairy-tale castles that had rosy pink, light
blue, deep green, or palest turquoise walls and towers.
Even ice floes as flat as pancakes intrigued him. They
edged together to form ever growing jigsaw
formations. Then along came fierce gusts of wind to
shatter them, sending rafts of ice chasing after one
another, or butting and smashing together like boxers
in the ring.

It was just as well that David had an intense
interest in ice. In the course of his first winter in North
America, an exceptionally cold one, he came face to
face with it every day. In his words,

"All the wood that could be collected for fuel gave us only one fire in
the morning and another in the evening. The rest of the day, if bad
weather, we had to walk in the guard room with our heavy coats of
dressed beaver; but when the weather was tolerable we passed the

day in shooting grouse [ptarmigan]. The interior walls of the house were covered with rime [frost] to the thickness of four inches, pieces of which broke off, to prevent which we wetted the whole extent and made it a coat of ice, after which it remained firm and added to the warmth of the house."

When the *Prince Rupert* finally anchored in the mouth of the Churchill River, approximately halfway along the western coast of Hudson Bay, David had truly arrived in a new world. There was nothing here to remind the recent student of the Grey Coat School, Westminster, London, of his "strolls to Spring Gardens and other places, where all was beauty to the eye and verdure to the feet." He was in a subarctic region, more rock than soil, littered by loose stones that hurt the feet, sodden with mile after mile of marshland, and hardly a tree to be seen. The first bitter breaths of winter were beginning to harden the land. By mid-November, the Churchill River, a fast-flowing waterway, was frozen solid. Spring tides ten to twelve feet in height would fail to make any impression on its icy prison. The welcome sight and sound of running water would not come again until the middle of June.

THE HUDSON BAY REGION, 1784

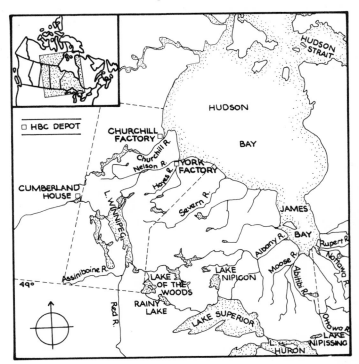

About five miles upriver, on the edge of a small rocky bay, was the Hudson's Bay Company depot of Churchill Factory, a cluster of log houses surrounded by a twelve-foot stockade. All around lay marsh and swamp, home to countless flocks of geese and ducks that filled human bellies throughout the year. The Company did not waste much money and shipping space transporting foodstuffs. Tea and sugar, flour and salt pork, were about all the supplies sent to the Bay. Employees had to live off the country by shooting game, netting fish, and snaring rabbits. If there was an occasional shortage of game or fish, then HBC men simply tightened their belts and learned to live on two meals a day — or just one. Indeed, it was no uncommon thing when journeying between Company posts, or when travelling inland to contact Indian customers, to have to get by for at least a day or two on nothing but strong, heavily sugared cups of tea. David learned this lesson very quickly, and he spent a lot of time practising musket shooting. The result was that he could usually be relied upon to bring something back for the supper pot.

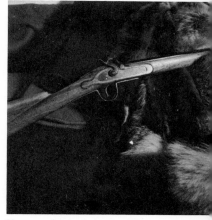

Very popular trade items with an Indian were a musket, lengths of cloth, and copper kettles. Why were these favourite purchases?

Except for going out to find game when the weather permitted, there really wasn't much for David to do. In his *Narrative*, memoirs written when he was an old man, he complained that it was the custom of the Hudson's Bay Company to

"send to the school in which I was educated to procure a Scholar who had a mathematical education to send out as Clerk.... To learn what? For all I had seen in their service neither reading nor writing was required. My only business was to amuse myself, in winter growling at the cold; and in the open season shooting Gulls, Ducks, Plover, and Curlews and quarrelling with Musketoes and Sand flies."

These lines reveal the self-centredness that David was to display at various points in his life. He had a habit of seeing things only from his own point of view. In fact, at this particular time the Company was trying to recover from a sudden shattering interruption of its normal peaceful existence: a French invasion of the Bay.

Britain and France had long been the worst of enemies. For centuries they had met in combat on European battlefields. By the eighteenth century, this rivalry had spread to India and North America. What we today call "frontier" or "brushfire" wars broke out several times on both continents. One result was that the Hudson's Bay Company, which had calmly started up business in 1670 in what was technically French territory, had suffered a number of raids on its Bay posts. But by 1763 the Company's future looked absolutely rosy. In the course of yet another brushfire war, the British defeated their opponents and also forced them to hand over official ownership of the entire northern half of North America — about three million square miles of real estate. (This wasn't bad going, because Britain already owned the thirteen colonies on the Atlantic coast of the continent — the future United States of America.) All the French could do was wait and watch for a chance of revenge. They thought they saw such an opportunity just two years before David Thompson arrived at Churchill Factory.

By this date, the fumbling, bumbling efforts of King George III of Great Britain and his advisers to defeat the rebellious townsfolk, farmers, and frontiersmen of the thirteen colonies were being laughed at by the rest of Europe. Britain was clearly losing the War of American Independence. The French decided that this was an excellent opportunity to attack the British Navy, which was badly strained by the twin tasks of shepherding convoys across the Atlantic and blockading ports on the Atlantic coast of North America to keep European supplies of war materials out of the colonists' hands. This decision was based more on sheer optimism than anything else: the British met the main French fleet in West Indian waters and blasted much of it out of existence. But several squadrons survived to roam the Atlantic in search of British merchant ships to plunder.

With a burning desire to avenge national honour, one particular trio of French warships sailed all the way to Hudson Bay to terrorize the Company and bring its trade to a standstill. They captured and gutted the then depot at the mouth of the Churchill, the huge, stone strongpoint of Fort Prince of Wales. Then they travelled another hundred or so miles farther south, stormed the important depot of York Factory, and burned it to the ground. When the three ships set sail for France, every last member of Fort Prince of Wales and of York Factory was a prisoner below decks.

The Churchill River fur trade conducted at Fort

Prince of Wales never really recovered from this disaster. It wasn't just that the Fort lay empty for a whole year, or that its huge stores of trade goods had been taken away as the spoils of war. The real damage was the terrible loss of prestige in the eyes of long-time customers. Even when the Prince of Wales' garrison, released from captivity, was sent out to build Churchill Factory the next year and resume trading operations, Indian trappers refused to believe that things were back to normal. They only had to look at the shattered cannon, burned gun-carriages, and broken walls of the fortress to marvel at the powerlessness of the British.

York Factory, which serviced HBC business on the Saskatchewan River, suffered a much lesser loss of prestige. Replacing a depot built of wood was easily and quickly done. In any case, there was a big difference between the fur trade at Churchill and that at York. The many rapids and falls of the Churchill River made it difficult for HBC men to travel inland. Thus Indians came down to Prince of Wales to trade. At York, HBC men had begun to journey inland via the much more navigable Saskatchewan River, trade with Indians, and bring furs back to the Bay.

But the French attack could not be shrugged off. It took time to reassemble men and supplies, contact traders living hundreds of miles inland on the

The depot of Fort Prince of Wales was built in the shape of a rough square, its sides being 300 feet from the tip of one arrow-headed bastion to the next. Every depot and fur post was made defensible. But why, in this one case, did the Hudson's Bay Company go to all the trouble of constructing a stone fortress?

Saskatchewan River, and convince customers that the
Company was back to stay. After all, for at least a year
after the French attack, the handful of HBC men
working inland had had no trade goods to offer
Indians. In most cases, these traders had lacked nets,
muskets, or ammunition with which to gather food.
They only survived by borrowing fishing and hunting
gear from their customers.

Small wonder David Thompson was ignored in all
the hustle of reorganizing things from scratch.
Everybody was too busy warehousing goods from the
Prince Rupert, repairing defective shipments (muskets
often arrived damaged or rusted, knives bent, and axe
handles broken), or scouring the countryside for food.

There was another reason why everybody was kept
pretty busy. David knew something about this,
although he did not quite understand what all the fuss
was about. He kept overhearing conversations between
veteran employees in which it seemed the Company's
troubles really had nothing to do with the French at all.
Sure, they had burned and looted. But this was just a
business hazard that happened every now and then.
The Company had survived this sort of thing several
times over in its 114-year history. In any case, the
French were gone and had no bases in North America.
No, the problem had nothing to do with hit-and-run
raids. It was persistent trade rivalry from *Britishers* in
the south that appeared to be the trouble.

The year David arrived at Churchill Factory, these
rivals were reported to be more numerous than ever.
They were muscling into the Company's business and
taking much of it away from HBC traders working
inland. The most aggressive were said to be those who
called themselves "Nor'Westers." Yet David's seniors
didn't seem to want to talk about these interlopers. In
fact, the officers at Churchill Factory positively
discouraged any questions from anybody about the
Nor'Westers. Why was HBC management being so
mysterious? What was it afraid of? David had to wait to
find out.

The First Step

It was a long winter. From the end of October to the beginning of May, every step beyond the palisade of Churchill Factory was made on snowshoes. Even within the depot the weather left no one doubtful about the season. For three days in December, a storm howled and raged out of the northeast, hurling snow against the twelve-foot stockade and then clear over it to fill the yard to depths of anywhere from six to ten feet. Walkways had to be shovelled out from house to house, and it was the end of April before a gradual thaw cleared the snow away.

Fond as he was of reading, David was essentially an outdoors type. Guard duty bored him, and he welcomed any opportunity to get away from the depot. He still had much to observe and learn.

In the early winter period, David often saw the polar bear prowling about "until the ice at the sea shore is extended to a considerable distance, when he leaves to prey on the Seal, his favourite food." He shrewdly noticed that polar bears were found only at or next the sea, never beyond the high-tide mark; thus, "keeping the line of the sea coasts, they appear more numerous than they really are." A polar bear skin stretched on a frame to dry was David's first introduction to one of these huge beasts. He measured it carefully and recorded a length of ten and a half feet. He also noted that a forepaw of another bear, kept by a fellow employee as a trophy, weighed all of 22 pounds, "a decent paw to shake hands with."

A tame polar bear was actually at Churchill Factory. He had been captured as a cub by some HBC whalers when they were out in the Bay in the summer in pursuit of a beluga, or white whale. At first "Bruin" had to be protected from the dogs at Churchill Factory but, as he grew larger and stronger, could keep them at bay with his powerful, clawed forepaws. Bruin was a great favourite with his sailor captors, who wrestled with him and allowed him some of their spruce beer ration. In winter, this beer froze, and the Company

THE CANADIAN WEST, 1785

substitute was a quart of molasses for every four men. Bruin dearly loved this sweet, treacly mess and lined up with his friends at the wine steward's shed to get his own special issue. One day, however, he and one of the stewards had quarrelled about something or other, and Bruin's punishment was to be severe — no molasses. The bear waited patiently until everybody in the depot had been served, then burst through the slowly closing door of the shed, shoved his head right into a hogshead of molasses, and marched out with the barrel still covering his face, molasses dripping down all over his furry body. He then sat down right in the middle of the depot and licked himself clean. Thereafter, no matter what quarrels any steward had with Bruin, he always got his ration of molasses.

An incident involving a polar bear gave David Thompson a valuable insight into Indian life. One November day, he and a companion had been out snaring hares, shooting grouse, and checking traps set for martens, foxes, and that craftiest of furred animals, the wolverine. As they hauled three sleds piled with game back to the depot in the evening, the boys kept one eye open for "our enemy, the polar bear." Hearty eaters, the animals had acquired the habit of helping themselves to whatever game HBC hunting parties had found. When the friends got back, they discovered that two men and an Indian woman, out on a similar mission, had not returned.

It turned out that these three had decided to camp out for the night. They pitched tent, a canvas structure shaped like a bell tent with the top cut off to let smoke out, and began frying ptarmigan for supper. Attracted by the savoury smell, a polar bear arrived and marched round and round the tent until it found the opening and stuck its head and shoulders inside. One of the men, John Bellam, panicked and scrambled up the tent pole. His companion, William Budge, snatched up an unloaded musket and hit the bear over the head with it several times; the woman grabbed an axe and did likewise. Between them, they drove the bear outside. Budge looked around, found a loaded fowling-piece, and was skilled or lucky enough to kill the bear. Bellam now wanted to come down from the smoky top of the tent, but the woman, axe in hand, heaped more wood on the fire and threatened to brain him if he did. He

Reconstructing a canot de maître *or Nor'Wester, freight canoe identical in size to those that journeyed between Montreal and Grand Portage on Lake Superior. How many tons of cargo could this vessel carry? What kinds of goods were transported?*

It has been said that the culture of Indians living in the subarctic reflects their eternal need to survive a harsh environment. How do these illustrations back up this statement?

begged hard, but she refused to let him come down. Budge snatched the axe out of her hand, and Bellam escaped being barbecued. "But," as David records, "she never forgave him, for the Indian woman pardons man for everything but want of courage. This is her sole support and protection, for there are no laws to defend her."

And so the long gloomy winter slowly passed. Everyone looked eagerly forward to the summer although, in northern latitudes of North America, the price of summer can be a terrible one—mosquitoes. The air is thick with them. They are constant companions, day and night. Every fur trader or explorer who kept a diary has written many bitter remarks about the ever present mosquito. David complained that smoke was no relief, for "they can stand more smoke than we can." The narrow windows of Churchill Factory were practically choked with the insects, and "they trod each other to death in such numbers, we had to sweep them out twice a day."

But all this did nothing to dull the boy's intense curiosity about the winged horror that inflicted itchy bumps all over his body. He borrowed a magnifying glass and a microscope to find out for himself how a mosquito operates. After a bit of trial and error (and some personal discomfort), David discovered that the insect's proboscis was composed of two distinct parts: a three-sided, black, sharp-pointed structure and, inside this, a round white tube. The first is used to puncture the skin and draw it back; the tube is then applied to the wound, and blood sucked through it. Thus, the bite is "two, distinct operations, but so quickly done as to feel as only one."

David went on from there to investigate preventative measures. A sailor, finding swearing no use, covered his face with tar, but mosquitoes stuck to it in such numbers that he was blinded. And the tickling of their wings, David said, was worse than their bites. He decided oil was the only remedy. All animals suffered equally, he found, almost to the point of madness. Well-feathered birds were attacked about the eyes and neck. Dogs rolled themselves howling on the ground. Barking and snapping on all sides in the mosquito season "the Fox seems always to be in a fighting humour." David was forced to the conclusion that "Hudson's Bay is certainly a country that Sinbad the Sailor never saw, as he makes no mention of Muskitoes."

In September, 1785, a year after his arrival at the Bay, David Thompson set off on the first stage of his many wanderings. He was ordered to join the garrison at York Factory, 150 miles southeast of Churchill. With two Indians as guides, his entire equipment a musket, some ammunition, and a blanket, he was told to walk to the York depot and report there for duty.

It was an unexciting experience. On one side was the muddy shoreline of Hudson Bay, on the other the marshes and swamps typical of the region. Each day the trio passed groups of polar bears snoozing on the mud flats, their heads close together and their bulky bodies lying as "radii from a centre." Rarely did a bear bother to lift its head and look them over. The only really interesting thing to David was the amazing number of wildfowl in the marshes. He would never again in his life see so many geese, an important item on the menu of any Hudson's Bay post. As always, his mind seethed with questions. He had heard that many of these birds nested 2,700 miles to the south at the mouth of the Mississippi. But how did they make the journey to and fro with such precision? Instinct, he was told. But what was instinct? He was forced to the conclusion that it was "a property of mind that has never been defined. The Indian believes the geese are directed by the Manitou [spirit] who has the care of them. Which of the two is right?"

Life at York Factory turned out to be no different from that at Churchill. The best shots — David was one — were off in the marshes most days bagging game, which would be salted and thus preserved for later use, or setting traps. Some servants, as HBC personnel were called, felled trees and sawed wood for the winter stockpile. Others cleaned and pressed furs or kept the account books. Still others worked at their trades as carpenters or blacksmiths. And York was just about as cold and damp as Churchill. Some days, the temperature dropped to 85 degrees below freezing.

In the course of his second year at Hudson Bay, David was greatly relieved to be ordered inland. He was assigned to an experienced trader as clerk, or writer. More trading centres had to be built and manned. More Indians had to be contacted and persuaded to become trappers. Although he did not know it, David really had the Nor'Westers to thank for this. These super-aggressive salesmen were taking more and more trade away from the Hudson's Bay Company, which only had two posts along the entire length of the mighty Saskatchewan River. Bit by bit, he began to learn a few things about his rivals and their organization, the North West Company.

The North West Company was created about ten years before David arrived at Churchill Factory. Its name is confusing because this organization was actually composed of several Montreal fur companies. In fact, this was no properly constituted "company" in the modern sense. It was nothing more than a trading name used by a loose association of men who worked together to get hold of and market more furs than anybody else in the trade. And this is exactly what the North West Company managed to do for almost fifty years.

The fur trade existed for several centuries because of a persistent fashion in men's hats. Kings, princes, nobles, wealthy merchants, bankers, and even senior army and navy officers would never dream of appearing in public without wearing a beaver hat. How do you explain this persistent fashion?

"Continental" cocked hat (1776)

Clerical (eighteenth century)

The fur trade based on Montreal was run by a mixture of explorer-traders and businessmen who had taken over the French fur trade exactly as they found it — language, transportation and routes, and operating methods. They knew a good thing when they saw it. All they had to do was put more effort and more money into what was obviously a paying proposition.

The late 1760s and early 1770s were pioneer days on the Saskatchewan River, when a resourceful man could make a small fortune from just two seasons of fur trading. Why? Because during the bitter, bloody campaigns of the Seven Years' War (1756-1763) in North America, the French, striving desperately to retain a foothold on the continent, had been unable to spare men or money to maintain trade at their western fur posts. Thus an extremely profitable market was waiting to be exploited when the war ended. European aristocrats and the members of a growing middle class of bankers, merchants, and industrialists had been cut off from a major source of supply of the pelts — beaver in particular — from which their fashionable felt hats were made. And the Indians of the upper Great Lakes region and the Saskatchewan country had been deprived of the European goods — axes, chisels, knives, muskets, combs, mirrors, shawls, thread, needles — to which they had become accustomed by many years of commerce with the French. At the same time, the Hudson's Bay Company, accustomed to receiving large supplies of furs from Indians living either near the Bay or well north of the Saskatchewan, continued its policy of enticing these customers to trade at its saltwater depots. Indeed, the Company let fully a hundred years pass before building its first depot in the western interior, Cumberland House, on an island in the Saskatchewan River.

It was a mere half a dozen or so of these Montreal-based adventurers and fur merchants, however, who had expanded the trade even farther than the French had done. In the process, these men discovered a remote region called Athabasca, several hundred miles north and west of the Saskatchewan River. The subarctic Athabasca country was to become a treasure house for anyone working in the fur trade. Here, winter lengthened to eight or nine months of the year, so furs were therefore heavy, rich, and glossy. When this handful of men saw and handled the magnificent pelts brought from Athabasca, each of them was struck by the same thought: with superb furs such as these, a man could make a fortune several times over. The result was a prolonged effort by these traders and merchants to make Athabasca their exclusive sales territory. In fact, they were not content

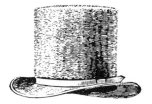

The Regent (1825)

The D'Orsay (1820)

The Wellington (1812)

The Paris Beau (1815)

to keep just Athabasca to themselves. They tried to take over the entire *pays d'en haut,* the high or upper country, the name the French had given to all the lands beyond the Great Lakes. So several Montreal merchants established partnerships with each other and also with a number of "wintering partners," each firm's senior traders in the pays d'en haut. And all of them used the handy title of the North West Company to describe their common business activities.

From the beginning the North West Company was an immensely successful combination of experienced wintering partners — Nor'Westers as they proudly called themselves — and several well-financed Montreal fur companies. With few exceptions, Nor'Westers were men who displayed unrelenting opposition to anyone who was not of their number. They acted as if they *owned* the pays d'en haut. Whether competing with traders working for other Montreal companies or with the men from the Bay, they sometimes used Mafia-like tactics: threatened or actual violence (including killing several Montreal rivals), hijacking competitors' supplies of goods, and bribing, bullying, or intoxicating Indians into becoming customers. Indeed, many Nor'Westers effectively controlled groups of Indians by making them dependent upon handouts of liquor. If these tactics did not work, their colleagues in Montreal sometimes neutralized competition by bringing rivals into the Company as fellow partners and giving them a share of the profits. Ruthless, powerful, but outwardly respectable, the North West Company was one of the earliest examples of "Big Business" in North America.

The men from the Bay referred to their rivals as the "Pedlars from Quebec" because they often took goods all the way to Indian encampments and there haggled for furs. But their contempt was misplaced. Nor'Westers were a breed of men who thrived on cut-throat competition and regularly engaged in price wars. Their only concern was to grab up pelts by the hundreds, if not the thousands. It didn't matter how many Indians were cheated or robbed outright in the process. It was of no consequence whether a Nor'Wester used liquor, guile, or threats — or all three — provided that he could send back canoe loads of fur to his sponsors in Montreal.

David Thompson found out he'd joined a company that had managed to outlast many years of competition from French fur traders, but was unable to handle these newcomers. Englishmen and Scotsmen — but mostly Scotsmen — coolly set up trading posts and depots all over lands granted by the British Crown to the "Governor and Company of Adventurers of England trading into Hudson's Bay." The interlopers were even doing business in the woods and marshes immediately south of Hudson Bay and James Bay, right on the Company's doorstep!

David was badly puzzled by all this information. These weren't Frenchmen. These were Britishers. And they were trading with licences issued annually by British officials in Quebec City and competing with a British corporation. But wasn't the Hudson's Bay Company supposed to enjoy, by royal decree, sole rights to all trade and commerce in what was called Rupert's Land, that is, in all the lands whose waters drained into Hudson Bay?

It was all too complicated to decide. And a bit boring, too. So David spent as much time as possible reading in the small room allotted to him, "without the least article of furniture except a hard bed."

Chapter 3 The Apprentice Trader

In the summer of 1786, equipped with the customary trunk, shoes, shirt, a musket, powder, and a tin pot (his drinking cup), the sixteen-year-old youth set off westward.

David's boss followed the turbulent Hayes River route to Lake Winnipeg. It was hard going. Paddling was useless. Loaded with 800 pounds of cargo, provisions, and personal belongings, each canoe had to be, as fur traders put it, "tracked" or "lined" upstream. Leaving one man on board to steer, the remainder of each crew shouldered a long, strong rope attached to the bow of their canoe and laboriously hauled it through the fast-flowing waters. In the heat of late July, stumbling bare-footed over a stony river bed was bad enough without also being tormented by hungry mosquitoes. Their hands fully occupied with the tracking line, the men's only protection were wide, floppy, cotton hats, which could be violently shaken to ward off their bloodthirsty attackers.

A month later, they had part-paddled, part-walked all the way to the drier, higher country on the edge of the prairies, close to where the North and South Saskatchewan Rivers join to form the mainstream. Travel was now much easier. As David put it, "we marched [paddled] fourteen hours, averaging 25 miles a day." At the junction of the two rivers, the party turned off up the South Saskatchewan. Instead of the dark pine woods of the Bay region, David found himself in a grassy countryside dotted with clumps of poplar, aspen, white birch, and ash. The entire area echoed with the whistling and calls of hundreds of deer. "We often heard the butting of the stag horns, battling which should be lord of the herd of does."

Three days' journey up the South Saskatchewan, David learned where and how to build a fur post. There, two Montreal companies were already in business next door to each other. So the men from the

Bay promptly cleared ground about 80 yards upstream from the competition. This way, they might well be able to attract the first customers coming downstream.

Few fur posts became permanent trading centres. The combination of traders eager for pelts and Indians hungry for European goods soon cleared out a territory of all marketable skins. On average, a post was occupied for a couple of years and then abandoned. So the building erected was usually a strictly functional one, a log hut divided up into three rooms. The middle one, about 12 feet by 20, was used for storing goods, provisions, and furs. Another, smaller room was the "indian hall" where the trading was done (and where the trader and his clerk slept rolled up in buffalo robes on the split-log floor). At the opposite end of the hut was the "guardroom," or men's quarters, a sort of kitchen-cum-dining-hall and workshop. Canoes, sleds, and snowshoes were stored on the rough timber rafters. At either end of the hut were fireplaces and

A reconstructed store in a fur post. At the far end is a square space through which trading was conducted. The loaf-like items hanging from the roof are carrottes of leaf tobacco. Behind them hang red and crimson sashes. How many other trading items can you recognize?

chimneys made of mud mixed with chopped-up, coarse grass.

Despite fires that were kept going day and night, a fur post was a cold, damp place to spend the winter. A good way to keep warm was by stoking up one's own central heating system — by eating heartily. This was one reason why canoemen, who spent much of the trading season out of doors cutting and hauling wood, or ice fishing, or hunting, were well-fed. Each was given a daily ration of eight pounds of fish or its rough equivalent of five pounds of deer or buffalo meat.

Business was good that winter, and David learned much. His customers were Cree and Assiniboine,

The wife of an Indian trapper in northern Quebec hangs out beaver pelts to dry. How were beaver caught? How were other furred animals trapped?

"tall, manly-looking men, with prominent features, well-dressed in leather, with a bison robe, the women dressed in much the same manner. They were friendly to us, and by no means troublesome, our axes and tools lying about, yet no thing was stolen . . . we builded and finished everything with as much ease and safety as if we had been alone."

However, the Assiniboine were not entirely trustworthy. They had a passionate love of horses and were notorious for stealing them from other tribes. As David put it, "It is said of a Yorkshire man, 'Give him a bridle, and he will find a horse,' but these [Indians] will find both the bridles and the horses."

These Indians brought in some beaver pelts, but most of what they had to trade was wolf or fox furs. Even coyote and lynx skins, thin and difficult though they were to work with, were gladly accepted at the post. In exchange, customers favoured long clothing. One of the HBC men was a tailor and spent much of his time transforming bolts of cloth into knee-length coats. HBC brandy was another popular purchase. David had not yet acquired the hatred of liquor that was to become a marked characteristic of his later years, so he merely deplored the fact that he could only water the brandy down twice before selling it. A little way downstream, he noted that his opponents brought in "high wines," a concentrated mixture of wine and rum or whisky, "to which four times the quantity of water was added to make grog for the Indians." But as David himself witnessed, what an Indian and his wife really desired were such common European household conveniences as cotton thread and scissors, blankets, and a kettle. This was even

Copper kettles and cloth, popular trading items

Plains Indians were dependent for almost all their needs on the buffalo. In what ways did they utilize this animal?

more obvious to him a year later, when he spent the winter, not at a post, but in an Indian encampment.

The ice broke up on the South Saskatchewan River in mid-April. As soon as the winter's take in furs had been loaded on board, the canoes set off on their long journey back to York Factory. But on the way downriver past Cumberland House, the sole HBC inland depot, David was re-routed up the north branch of the Saskatchewan. He was ordered to join a party of five HBC men who would winter at a Piegan camp. Their instructions were to learn the Indians' language and, in the process, somehow persuade them to give up their reputedly warlike habits for the more peaceful and profitable activity of trading pelts. And so in the fall of 1787, David found himself trudging southwest across the apparently endless prairies and leading a horse loaded with trade goods. David said that he had so much commercial baggage to take along, as well as his few personal belongings — a spare cotton shirt, a leather coat, and a buffalo robe — that he was obliged to walk most of the way.

Fur traders always referred to their canoe trips as "marching." But march David literally did, day in, day out, for several weeks on end "over extensive plains with patches of woods in places." He started out in what is now west-central Saskatchewan and ended up in southwestern Alberta with "the Rocky Mountains in sight like shining white clouds on the horizon . . . their immense masses of snow appeared above the clouds and formed an impassible barrier, even to the Eagle." On the Bow River, somewhere in the vicinity of the modern city of Calgary, David and his companions came face to face with a band of Piegans. "Some of their scouts had seen us, but could not say who we were. They were well mounted and armed with bows and quivers of arrows."

It is difficult to say who was more curious or more suspicious, the Piegans or the HBC men. Few of these Indians had ever seen a European before. And with the exception of James Gady, the leader of the expedition, no one had met those members of the Blackfoot nation. Like David, the other HBC personnel only had first-hand experience of the Cree and the Assiniboine. The Cree had long been friends and advisers to the Company. Some of them, the Woods Cree as they were called, had moved away from their original homeland of forest and lake immediately south of Hudson Bay to become what amounted to HBC agents in the vast forest that sprawls across the northern portions of what we call Manitoba, Saskatchewan, and Alberta. But the Piegan were a warrior society, nothing if not aggressive, and well-known for the ferocity with which they held their lands and fought off intruders.

The handful of traders had nothing to worry about. They were received as welcome guests and given "two horse-loads of fat cow meat." Just as important, the initial effect on the Piegans of trade goods was something to behold. Time and time again, David was to observe this delighted reaction:

"everything is carried on by barter profitable to both parties but more so to the Indians than to us. We took from them furrs [sic] of no use to them, and which had to pass through an immense distance of freight and risks before they could be sold in the market of London. See the wife of an Indian sewing their leather clothing with a pointed, brittle bone, or a sharp thorn, and the time and trouble it takes. Show them an awl or a strong needle, and they will gladly give the finest Beaver or Wolf skin they have to purchase it. When the tents remove, a steady, careful old man or two of them are entrusted with the fire, which is carried in a rough wooden bowl with earth in it and carefully led to the place of the [next] camp . . . a flint and steel saves all this anxiety and trouble . . . tobacco was the great luxury and, like money, commanded all things. Iron heads for their arrows are in great request, but above all guns and ammunition."

Trade was encouragingly brisk. With the Piegan, blue beads bought most furs because "the young men

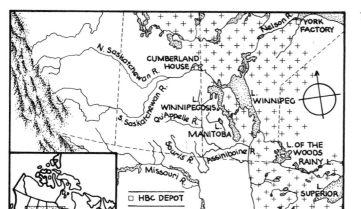

THE PRAIRIES

purchased them to make presents to the young
women." But, as the years went by, all the fur
companies discovered to their cost that, with the
exception of muskets and ammunition, the Blackfoot
nation couldn't care less about fur trapping. To them,
hunting buffalo and raiding other Indians' horse herds
was much more manly work — and much more fun.

The six traders separated into pairs to stay in
different teepees. David was fortunate enough to live
in the home of an old man called Sarkamappee, who
was actually a Plains Cree in origin. Sarkamappee was
delighted to discover that his guest had a working
knowledge of his language. (The Blackfoot, like the
Cree, belonged to a large group of Indians who spoke
the Algonkian tongue, so conversation between the old
warrior and the young trader was fairly easy.)
Sarkamappee had many stories to tell. He was so old
he could remember when wild horses, descendants of
those brought to the New World by the Spaniards, first
appeared on the prairies. Sarkamappee and his Piegan
friends had thought them *mis-stu-tims* ("big dogs").

Listening to his host almost every evening for four
months, David acquired more knowledge and
understanding of Indian ways than many a trader
picked up in a lifetime. One of the most important
things he learned was that Indians and Europeans
have very different views as to what life is all about.

"Indians can bear great fatigue but not hard labour. They would rather walk six hours over rough ground than work one hour with the pick-axes and spade. The labour they perform is mostly in an erect posture, as working with the ice chisel piercing holes through the ice [to fish] or through a beaver house. And naturally they are not industrious; they do not work from choice but from necessity . . . the civilized man has many things to tempt him to an active life; the Indian has none and is happy sitting still and smoking his pipe."

He learned of their kindness and courtesy to each other, the help given the sick, and the strong sense of communal sorrow felt at the death of any of their number. David was particularly impressed by the great care and tenderness with which children were brought up. They were seldom punished; the constant company and admonition of the old people provided a child's early education. He noted, too, the simple, generally held belief in the "Great Manitou," the Spirit of Spirits, who left men and women free to decide how to behave themselves but thoughtfully provided earth, water, fire, and all the animals for mankind's comfort and use — provided that certain hunting rituals were scrupulously observed.

Spring came, and it was time to rejoin the Company on the North Saskatchewan River. David said a reluctant goodbye to his fatherly host and set out on the long trek back to his starting point, a fur post just a little way west of the junction of the North and South Saskatchewan Rivers that had the grand title of Manchester House. (In the trade, it was quite a common habit to give important-sounding names to what were little more than log shanties.)

David would remember Manchester House as long as he lived. Here, two days before Christmas that year, he stumbled down the river bank and broke his right leg. The accident changed the whole course of his life.

The Young Chapter 4
Explorer

David had a miserable time for several months. The bone could not have been properly set because the leg was slow to heal. When canoes laden with furs for York Factory went down the Saskatchewan in early 1789, he went with them. But, even with splints and crutches, the pain and discomfort were too much. He would obviously not be able to cope with the many portages between Lake Winnipeg and Hudson Bay. David had to be left just a few miles downstream at Cumberland House. Here he passed the summer with two men to look after him.

About all David could do was sit at the river's edge and fish for sturgeon, which he says was "too rich for my state of health." But, ever the perceptive observer, he called it the "Water Hog" — meaning a good, fat source of food. Fresh or frozen, it was the staple food of traders working in the vast pine-and-birch forest north of the prairies. David noted from personal experience in later years that "whatever sturgeon flesh was not required for the day is laid by in a hoard and with all care is seldom more than enough for the winter."

It was in the fall of that year that David's career was radically changed. He was still sickly and still moving about with difficulty. But when the canoes returned from York Factory, they brought with them an HBC employee called Philip Turnor, who had been ordered by the governors of the company to find and map a route to the fur riches of Athabasca. In David's words,

"This was a fortunate arrival for me, as Mr. Turner [sic] was well versed in mathematics, was one of the compilers of the nautical almanacs, and a practical astronomer. Under him I regained my mathematical education . . . and thus learned practical astronomy under an excellent master of the science."

David Thompson was never the same again after that winter of instruction. From that time on, he set about exploring and mapping much of the Canadian

West. And it was Turnor who launched him on his amazing career as a surveyor and geographer. From Turnor, Thompson received all he was ever to know of advanced mathematics, astronomy, and field surveying. Turnor instructed the young man in the use of the telescope, the chronometer, the compass, and the thermometer. He also taught him to handle the sextant, the tables of the "Nautical Almanak," and the artificial (mercury) horizon. As for Thompson, surveying became as normal an act as breathing.

That winter of 1789, he made a series of observations of the sun and the stars in order to determine the exact latitude and longitude of Cumberland House. He finally decided that its location was 53 degrees, 56 minutes, 44 seconds north latitude and 102 degrees, 13 minutes west longitude — almost identical to that which it occupies on any authoritative map today. In addition, he began to keep the first of

TWO ROUTES INTO ATHABASKA

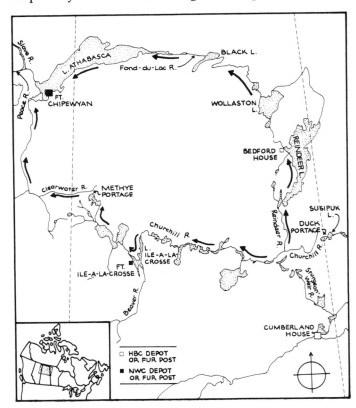

many journals in which his principal daily entries were temperature readings, notes on wind direction and force, and general remarks on the weather. From 1790 until he left the West in 1812, David Thompson did almost as much surveying as trading. There was no river or lake he travelled that he did not survey — and survey again if his journeyings took him over the same waters. There was no post or depot where he stayed whose latitude and longitude he did not plot — and if he went there again, he took fresh observations in order to check his earlier figures.

Two years after that memorable winter at Cumberland House, Thompson's apprenticeship ended. He immediately received an offer from the Company of a contract for three years at £15 (about $150) per annum in a letter describing his employment as "a surveyor and trader." Indeed, the London authorities went so far as to say that "every information that can tend to form a good Survey and Map of the Country Inland will always be particularly acceptable to us." A salary, small though it was, and promotion to the status of trader were pleasant changes from simply being fed, clothed, and instructed. However, there was little else for him to feel cheerful about. He was unable to get much exploring done.

The reasons for his disappointment had nothing to do with Thompson. The basic one was, of course, the Nor'Westers. Some of these master salesmen were now invading what HBC men had long considered their finest trading territory, the "Muskrat Country," a heavily forested, water-logged but beaver-rich region that lay west of York Factory between the Churchill and Nelson Rivers. Another difficulty, the conflicting decisions of the London governors of the Company, the men in charge of Churchill and York Factories, and William Tomison, the man in charge of inland trading along the Saskatchewan, did nothing to improve the situation. Unlike the North West Company's wintering partners, who met some of their Montreal colleagues each summer at Grand Portage on Lake Superior and worked out together sales strategy and tactics, the Hudson's Bay Company was crippled by the fact that there was no such quick, clear communication between

The restored "Great Hall" at Grand Portage, where North West Company executives met each summer to settle matters of salaries and profits, promotions and appointments, trade policies and expansion plans. Grand Portage was a depot, so what other buildings would it contain?

HBC executives and their sales managers. Once a year a ship called at Churchill Factory, at York Factory, and other depots on the Bay to offload trade goods, take on board bales of furs, and exchange reports and letters. So there was a time lag of 12 months in the information passed back to London and orders sent out from London. In between times, the commanders at Churchill and York and William Tomison made whatever decisions seemed best at the time.

For David Thompson, the result was a series of frustrations. In 1791, the year he was promoted to trader, he spent twelve months at York Factory doing what amounted to clerical work. In 1792, he was in charge of a trading party just north of the Saskatchewan River (where he consoled himself by making lunar observations to help work out the longitude of several locations). His next assignment did delight him: he was ordered to find a way into Athabasca. But after spending much of the summer on the Churchill River — one waterway that led to his goal — trying to find Indian guides, he had to give up and return to the Bay. Characteristically, he surveyed as he journeyed, mapping the river and even plotting the locations of Nor'Wester posts. He returned inland to spend the winter trading on the North Saskatchewan. In 1795, he returned to York via a roundabout northern route that added to his knowledge of the many waters draining down to Hudson Bay. But that winter, Thompson was sent back to the Muskrat Country. Here, he was thoroughly irritated and disgusted to find himself competing for furs not only with Nor'Westers, but also with HBC men from Churchill Factory.

At last, in 1796, he finally got the chance to attempt a major exploration. His target was Athabasca. Philip Turnor, who had tutored Thompson in survey work, had convinced the governors in London that the Company simply must establish itself in Athabasca. Turnor had managed to get there in the winter of 1791-92 and had seen something of the enormous profits being made by the Nor'Westers. They themselves calculated their annual trade there at about £50,000, which was approximately what they had been grossing each year in the West *before* they had even got to Athabasca. So strict orders were sent to Churchill

Much of the great boreal or northern forest where fur traders travelled and lived is in what geologists and others call the Canadian Shield. Why are so many Shield rivers broken by rapids and falls? What makes the Shield good country for hunting furred animals?

and York Factories to survey a route into this Eldorado.

The only known way into Athabasca, however, was to be avoided. This involved a long canoe trip to the headwaters of the Churchill River and then a lengthy portage over the height of land separating waters flowing to Hudson Bay from those draining down to the Arctic. This, the Company said, was far too long a detour to the west and north. There just had to be a shorter connection between Lake Athabasca — where the Nor'Westers had their depot of Fort Chipewyan — and Churchill and York Factories. The Company sternly reminded its servants that Chipewyans had

been coming down from Athabasca for years, apparently without using the 12-mile Methye Portage between Arctic and Bay waters. Someone had to find out the details of how these Indians did so.

Word of these orders was passed along to David Thompson and his immediate boss, Malcolm Ross, although it was late in the summer of 1796 before a real try for Athabasca got under way. Both men had spent the previous winter at different posts on Churchill waters. That year, Ross decided to escort their joint take in furs down to York, while his subordinate

Many a trader and his men had their canoe upset by rapids. Here, a team of researchers have recovered fur-trade goods from a whirlpool on a river in the Canadian Shield. What are these goods? How were they packed for transport?

pioneered a canoe route north to Lake Athabasca. And Thompson did find a way to the lake, although he nearly lost his life twice in the process.

Both episodes occurred on the return journey up the Black River. The first happened as Thompson and two Chipewyan guides navigated a steep fall with a rapid above and below it. They had portaged all their equipment a couple of hundred yards to a point above the uppermost rapid and were lining the empty canoe upstream while Thompson steered it clear of rocks and turbulent water. All was going well until the canoe suddenly sheered across the current.

"To prevent the canoe upsetting . . . I sprang to the bow of the canoe, took out my clasp knife, cut the line from the canoe . . . by this time I was on the head of the fall. All I could do was to place the canoe to go down bow foremost. In an instant the canoe was precipitated down the fall (twelve feet), and buried under the waves. I was struck out of the canoe and when I arose among the waves the canoe came on me and buried [me] beneath it . . ."

He managed to surface again by thrusting a foot against the stones of the river bed. Luckily, he came up next the canoe and grabbed it. Luckier still, the water at the foot of the fall was pushing the canoe into shallow water.

Thompson was alive but in bad shape. The flesh of his left foot had been torn off from the heel almost to the toes. His body was a mass of cuts and bruises. Worst of all, the powder, ammunition, and fishing gear were gone. The trio had no food, no means of getting any, and were a long way from home.

The journey back was a two-week nightmare of cold, hunger, and sickness. Blankets and spare clothing had been swept away in the upset, and portaging through thick undergrowth or tracking the canoe in waist-deep, rock-strewn shallows soon ripped their jackets and trousers to shreds. They were forced to tear up their tent to make rough cloaks for warmth during the chill nights. (Strips of tent made bandages for Thompson's torn foot.) On a diet of berries, they became steadily weaker each day.

Recalling that he had spotted an eagle's nest in a tree on the way downstream, Thompson kept looking for it and finally located the nest. In it were two eaglets, which the men eagerly killed and ate. Thompson and one of his companions consumed the masses of yellow fat they found when the birds were opened up, saving the flesh for a later meal. They did not know that the fat of a fish-eating bird can be rancid and dangerous to man, and both of them suffered violent attacks of dysentery for several days. By this time, Thompson was so sick and exhausted he says he just wanted to lie down and die.

The three explorers were only saved by a chance encounter with two Chipewyan families, who "gave us broth but would allow us no meat until the next day." With the loan of some deerskin clothing and moccasins, a few provisions, a flint and some ammunition, Thompson and his guides managed to get back in time to meet Malcolm Ross returning from York with a winter's supply of trade goods.

As things turned out that fall, Malcolm Ross was far from pleased with his assistant's summer exploration. True, he had found a way to and from the Athabasca country. But it did not sound like a *navigable* canoe route, that is, an easy route with few portages for canoes heavily laden with goods going one way and furs the other. Ross wanted to continue west on the Churchill River, swing northwest up and over the Methye Portage, and then north down the Athabasca River into the very heart of the region from which the Nor'Westers were extracting a bonanza of furs. But Thompson claimed to have found a shorter, more direct route north from the Churchill and somehow persuaded Ross to try it.

Nowhere in his own records does Thompson say that the result was a total failure. But Ross was forced to report to the Company in due course that, at one point on the trip, to get from one particular lake to another involved a portage of close to fifty miles! This was an impossible task for canoemen each carrying two 90-pound packs.

So once again the Hudson's Bay Company had failed to set up in business in Athabasca. As "Master to the Northward," the man picked to lead the Company's northward thrust, Ross would have to shoulder whatever blame was attached to this failure. It was now too late in the year to try any other way. Indeed, Ross would have to build a new post (Bedford House) in a region that seemed to him surprisingly lacking in game and hope he could keep an unusually large party—17 men and women—alive on whatever fish could be caught that winter.

Why did David Thompson make such a colossal blunder? He has left us no answer, nor have any of his colleagues. But the reason was probably his mania for surveying, which must have blinded him to all other considerations. His *Narrative* includes a chapter entitled "Trip to Lake Athabasca." Thompson mentions the need to find a way to this lake. Then he makes two casual but very interesting remarks. He says that, although he could find no other HBC man to accompany him on such a journey, "my curiosity to see unknown countries prevailed," hence his exploration with a couple of Indians who "happened to be there." After his description of the trip out and back, he adds, "It was always my intention to have fully surveyed this [Black Lake] and the Rein Deer's Lake [the modern Reindeer Lake], but the sad misfortune which happened in the lower part of the Black River, made me thankful to save our lives."

The second comment strongly suggests his real reason for returning in the fall to the scene of his summer's exploration.

It must have been a depressing winter for David Thompson. As usual, the post's chimneys were made of mud and coarse grass, but this time had been poorly constructed. "The huts were wretched with smoke, so that, however bad the weather, we were glad to leave the huts." December was the worst time.

"This dull month of long nights we wish to pass away; the country affords no tallow for candles . . . the light of the fire is all we have to work and read by. Christmas when it comes finds us glad to see it pass; we have nothing to welcome it with."

And, as his journal entries of temperature readings confirm, it was one of the coldest winters ever known in North America.

But his own thoughts must have troubled him much more. He'd made a complete fool of himself in his companions' eyes in his attempt to reach Athabasca. His superior, Malcolm Ross, had already given the Company a year's notice of his intention to retire. Thompson was his successor, the more so since the Company thought well of him. When his contract was renewed in 1794, his salary had jumped to £60 a year. But would the Company forgive his recent failure to act like a Master of the Northward?

Or was David Thompson more worried about the obviously pressing priority of trading over surveying? Only once in his later life would he willingly and wholeheartedly put trading before surveying. The rest of the time he put up with the necessity of it. Bartering for pelts was the means whereby he could earn a living, travel far and wide, and survey to his heart's content — all at one and the same time.

Nobody knows exactly why David Thompson did it, but he decided to quit the Hudson's Bay Company. On Tuesday, May 23, 1797, he left Bedford House and walked 75 miles to the nearest North West Company post. Here, he signed up with his former competitors.

One of these objects bears, on one side, the coat of arms of the Hudson's Bay Company. On the other are markings meaning that, in the Company's East Main District, the object was equal to half the pelt of an adult beaver pelt in prime condition. The other object has the head of King George IV of Great Britain on one side and the name of the HBC's great rival on the other. What were these objects? What were they used for?

Chapter 5 **Surveyor and Mapmaker**

David Thompson could not have joined the Nor'Westers at a better time. They had the men, money, and motivation to succeed. Just as important, they knew a good deal about the geography of Canada and how to turn it to their commercial advantage.

A Canadian prime minister once said, "If some countries have too much history, Canada has too much geography." A lot of this geography is water. Canada is made up of a higher proportion of fresh water than any other country on earth. And three-quarters of this water spills out through three huge drainage basins that are like gigantic saucers with low rims: the Great Lakes-St. Lawrence River system; the Saskatchewan River-Lake Winnipeg-Nelson River complex; and the Mackenzie River and its many tributary waters.

The Nor'Westers knew from their French predecessors and from their own travels that the rims, or heights of land, separating these basins could be crossed fairly easily. There was no great rise in height from Montreal all the way to Grand Portage on the north shore of Lake Superior, nor from Grand Portage another 2,000 miles inland to Fort Chipewyan on Lake Athabasca.

They had also discovered that a chain of interconnecting lakes and rivers gave access from Montreal to just about any place in the interior of North America. A canoe could be (and still can be) paddled almost all the way from Montreal to the Gulf of Mexico, to Hudson Bay, or to the Arctic Ocean. This explains many a fur-trade route. This is the reason why, once across the height of land about 100 miles north of their depot at Grand Portage, the Nor'Westers fanned out through almost every region west and north of Lake Superior. From Grand Portage, they paddled and portaged their way to man 100 fur posts in what are now the state of Minnesota, the provinces of Manitoba, Saskatchewan, and Alberta, and the

Thompson used this type of sextant to calculate the sun's altitude. Using this information along with the tables of a nautical almanac, he could then work out the latitude of his location.

Northwest Territories. With David Thompson's help, the Nor'Westers were destined to extend their operations into today's province of British Columbia and the states of Montana, Idaho, and Washington.

Despite their considerable knowledge of Canada's geography, the Nor'Westers needed Thompson's skills as a surveyor and mapmaker. One of the clauses of the peace treaty that ended the war between King George III and his rebellious American subjects established a common boundary in the east between British North America and the newly formed republic of the United States. This directly affected the North West Company. After passing more or less through the middle of the Great Lakes, this border followed the Pigeon River (just a few miles east of Grand Portage itself) inland from Lake Superior to the Lake of the Woods. It then continued west along the 49th parallel of latitude until, as the peacemakers imagined, it met the headwaters of the Mississippi River. Sooner or later, Americans would force the Company to abandon Grand Portage, which stood on United States soil. But there were many Nor'Wester posts west and north of Grand Portage. Which of them was also in American territory? Which would have to be moved and which abandoned?

So the Company's orders to the man appointed its "Surveyor and Map Maker" were very businesslike. Survey the 49th parallel of latitude to find out where it ran, especially in the Red River region where there were several Nor'Wester posts. Determine the exact position of all Company posts visited in relation to the 49th parallel. If possible, extend surveying to the upper Missouri River country, which was thought to be south of the 49th parallel and, therefore, not British territory. The Mandan Indians living there were said to practise agriculture, but had long been known to possess good-quality furs.

On a hot day early in August, Thompson climbed up the nine-mile portage trail to its western end at the Pigeon River (hence the French term, *Le Grand Portage*). Here, he found his canoemen waiting patiently for him. They squatted or lolled on the ground beside their *canots du nord*. Dressed in moccasions, deerskin leggings, breechclouts, and loose shirts or deerhide

A chronometer helped him to calculate the longitude of his position.
    What are latitude and longitude? How are they used to pinpoint any place on the earth's surface?

jerkins, their hair hanging down over their shoulders to give them some protection from mosquitoes, they looked like a band of desperadoes. These were some of the famous *hommes du nord*, or northmen, the most experienced, the boldest, and the hardiest of the hundreds of voyageurs employed by the Company. It was northmen who took over the chores of paddling and portaging beyond Grand Portage and transported goods and furs to and from the many posts in the pays d'en haut. Without the northmen's skills, strength, and stamina, such famous Nor'Westers as Alexander Mackenzie, Simon Fraser, and David Thompson would have found it even more difficult — perhaps impossible — to find a way to the Arctic Ocean or through the mountains to the Pacific coast.

Aboard one canoe in a "brigade" commanded by a *bourgeois*, or wintering partner, Thompson set off up the Pigeon River. He was following the historic route into the pays d'en haut taken by French explorers at least a hundred years earlier. In the 600 miles of jumbled granite and dense timber that lay between Grand Portage and Lake Winnipeg, almost every portage, river, and lake bore a French name, casual legacies left behind by unknown *coureurs de bois*.* Nor'Westers called this route the "Northwest Road." (Fur traders called all canoe routes "roads," just as they referred to all canoe trips as marches.)

It was a rough road. The first 150 miles were interrupted by 29 carrying-places. These varied from a mile to less than the length of a canoe. One of them, known as the Stairway Portage, was crossed by using handholds cut into rock. And all these trails were over ground thick with granite boulders and stones, choked with tangled underbrush, and infested by hungry mosquitoes. The next 250 miles were fairly easy, a succession of beautiful grey-green lakes, rimmed with ancient rock and tall trees. But everyone in the brigade knew that the last 200 miles were bad — the long length of the Winnipeg River, which even the carefree voyageurs respectfully called the "White River." Its roaring, tortured waters necessitated twenty-six portages, and its navigable rapids were awesome enough to make even a northman's heart hammer with fear.

Once on the shallow, wind-tossed waters of "Lake

*"Runners of the woods": individual fur traders who were refused — or did not bother to seek — the trading licences issued by the government of New France.

Winnipeg or the Sea, so-called by the natives from its size," Thompson left the brigade and headed for the western shore. He followed a river across to the next lake west (Manitoba) and then swung north to reach another lake (Winnipegosis). As always, he charted every mile he travelled. Thompson was now once again on the northeastern edge of the "Great Plains" that start at "the Gulf of Mexico and extend northward to the latitude of fifty four degrees, where these plains are bounded by the forests of the north. On the east they are bounded by the Mississippe [sic] River . . . and on the west by the Rocky Mountains." In fact, he was quite close to the scene of his first trading experience, the South Saskatchewan River.

Obtaining horses at a local Nor'Wester post, he and a colleague rode far south over the plains, making occasional side trips to check the position of various Company trading centres. (His calculations told him he was still north of the 49th parallel.) He stopped off at one of these, McDonnell's House, to spend several days making inked copies of his pencilled journal, survey notes, and sketch maps. He made a habit of sending these inked reports to Grand Portage via a courier system the Company maintained between major posts and the depot.

It was now late November. Chill winds sweeping across the Great Plains announced that winter was on the way. But this did not worry Thompson. He was too interested in the "ancient agricultural Indians" living in villages a mere 250 miles away on the Missouri River to be deterred by a little thing like bad weather. Borrowing an interpreter, a guide, seven northmen, and a few trading items from John McDonnell, the Nor'Wester in charge, Thompson rode on south in search of the Mandan villages.

The first morning out the temperature was minus 27 degrees, and "the men thought it too cold" to leave their tents and travel over the open plains. The next morning the temperature was minus 32 degrees and four degrees colder still by 9 p.m. Nonetheless, Thompson and some of the men had to turn out and hunt down a couple of buffalo so that there would be something to eat. The thermometer recorded minus 37 degrees the day after, and there was a roaring,

Voyageurs were a hardbitten and hardworking lot. But they were also very superstitious. Thompson records that his men were convinced that the pass he was looking for in the mountains was the "haunt of the mammoth," reputedly a huge hairy, monstrous-looking animal. Were his men referring to what some people today call Sasquatch? What is a Sasquatch?

screaming gale that chilled everyone to the bone. They finally got going five days after leaving McDonnell's House and endured several snowstorms, including one during which a man was lost for a time and nearly froze to death. Many of the usual landmarks were blotted out by snowdrifts, but Thompson's work with telescope and compass managed to keep them all on course. However, it took them 33 days to complete a journey that was normally accomplished in ten.

He spent a happy month visiting several Mandan groups, filling his journals with notes on their dome-shaped, sodded homes: the internal design of these communal dwellings; and the fruit and vegetables stored for the winter — maize, pumpkins, beans, and melons. He admired the clean, neat appearance of his hosts, describing them as "of a stature fully equal to Europeans . . . well-limbed, the features good, the countenance mild and intelligent." He disapproved of the famous Mandan dancing women, "all courtesans, a set of handsome, tempting women." In fact, he was horrified to discover they sometimes indulged in indiscriminate love-making. "This the men with me knew, and I found it was their sole motive for their journey." But he was honest enough to admit that the Europeans who had hitherto visited these villages had not been outstanding examples of virtue themselves. The morality of Indians, Thompson decided, was much more concerned with the necessity of maintaining general law and order. "The crimes they hold to be avoided are theft, treachery, and murder." Murder was the worst sin.

Undaunted by the perils and pains of his December journey, Thompson set out in January, 1798, on the return journey. The weather was almost as cold and stormy as on the outward leg, and it took him and his party 24 days to get back to McDonnell's House (which he re-calculated was just north of the 49th parallel). He paused here long enough to check the notes and observations he had made on side trips up and down the Missouri and to make a map. Then he began to search for the headwaters of the Mississippi. At Thompson's request, John McDonnell supplied him with three northmen, an Indian guide, and three dog sleds loaded with provisions.

A typical page from one of David Thompson's journals. What did he record in the first six columns?

Trudging along on snowshoes this time, Thompson traced the Assiniboine River east to where it joins the Red River, the site of modern Winnipeg. Then he turned south and marched up the broad frozen Red. Its windings prompted him to write, "An Indian compared the devious course of the river to a spy, who went here and there and everywhere to see what was going on in the country." By mid-March, he had reached a Company post at the mouth of the Pembina River. Finding it to be a little way south of the 49th parallel, he politely advised the manager, Charles Chaboillez, to relocate a few miles north. After a week's rest, Thompson plodded on south up the Red (coming upon a post at the mouth of a tributary), turned east up Red Lake River and, when he came to one of its feeder streams, found another post (Cadotte's House). He noted that all the waterways he came across were northbound. He had yet to cross the height of land that separates waters flowing down to Hudson Bay from those of the Mississippi and other Plains rivers that empty into the Gulf of Mexico far to the south.

The first rains of spring were turning the snow to mush, and every day the weary travellers were soaked

This is the Lake Superior section of David Thompson's "MAP of the NORTH-WEST TERRITORY of the PROVINCE OF ONTARIO...", 1814. The map does not name Grand Portage or the falls of Sault Ste. Marie. But where is each location?

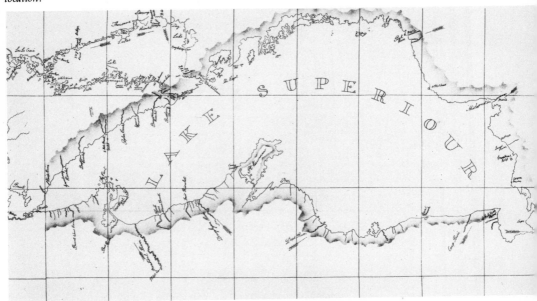

to the skin. Even at night around a roaring campfire they could not seem to get dry. And the going was very rough. "The ankles and knees were sprained with the weight of wet snow on each snow shoe, for the snow was not on firm ground but supported by long grass." So Thompson led his men back to Cadotte's House to rest. Here, he enjoyed the company of Baptiste Cadotte, a Métis, and his "very handsome" wife, also born of French and Indian parents. Cadotte advised him to wait until the river ice broke up in a couple of weeks' time. This seemed a good idea to Thompson not because it was a chance to rest and relax, but an opportunity to observe the "workings of the climate of 48 degrees north, aided by the influence of the great and warm valley of the Mississippe, which was near to us."

Determined to find the source of the Mississippi, he made a fresh start eastward from Cadotte's post on April 9th, this time by canoe. Stalled again by ice nine days later, he built a sled and put the canoe and supplies on it. Then he and his four men (and the Indian wife of one of the men) harnessed themselves to the sled and hauled it 17 miles through rain and sleet until they came upon open water again (Lower Red Lake). On April 27th, after crossing a bewildering number of small lakes and brooks due south of Lower Red Lake, the party arrived at a lake (Turtle Lake) with a waterway exiting to the southwest. Thompson decided that this was the "source of the Mississippe."

He was wrong by a matter of a few miles. A generation later, it was decided that the source is Itasca Lake, a body of water just a little farther south and west. Not everyone agrees that this is correct. Some geographers today claim that the source is Little Elk Lake, a tiny body of water to the south of Turtle Lake. Thompson, however, was at least 100 miles below the border and had exposed the error of the diplomats in supposing that the 49th parallel crossed the headwaters of the mighty Mississippi.

Thompson headed southeast for some distance and then cut across country to the westernmost end of Lake Superior, finding three more posts on American soil in the course of this particular survey. He did not return right away to Grand Portage as he could have done

Alexander Mackenize (top) and William McGillivray, both executives of the North West Company, were good friends of long standing. Three years after Thompson met them at Sault Ste. Marie, they became the bitterest of enemies. Why?

with relative ease by following Superior's north shore for about 150 miles. His geographer's instinct sensed an opportunity. So he made his way down to the south side of Superior and surveyed this shoreline of almost 700 miles all the way east to the falls of Sault Ste. Marie. (Lake Superior waters pour over these falls on their way to Lakes Huron and Michigan.) Here, on May 28th,

"I had the pleasure of meeting Sir Alexander Mackenzie, the celebrated traveller who was the first to follow down the great stream of water flowing northward from the Slave Lake into the Arctic Sea, and which great river bears his name. . . . The next day the Honourable William McGillivray arrived. These gentlemen were the agents and principal partners of the North West Company; they requested me to continue the survey of the lake round the east and north sides to the Grand Portage . . ."

Thompson arrived back at Grand Portage on June 7th. He had been gone ten months and had completed almost 4,000 miles of surveying. Even Alexander Mackenzie, the famous explorer, was quite astounded and remarked that Thompson had performed more in ten months than he expected could have been done in two years.

WEST OF SUPERIOR

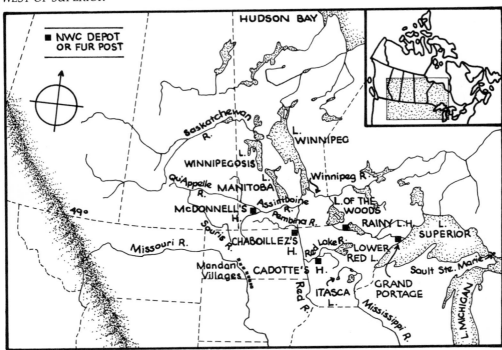

West of the Chapter 6
Mountains

His 4,000-mile journey by canoe, horse, and snowshoe
was just the beginning of Thompson's travels as a
Nor'Wester. In later years he would once again winter
alongside the Churchill River. He would return to the
Muskrat Country west of Hudson Bay. He would even
make several journeys into the Athabasca country.
Sometimes he was free to spend all his energy
exploring and surveying. As often as not, however, he
was in charge of trading parties and had much less
chance to follow his favourite occupation. Times were
changing. Year by year, the Hudson's Bay Company
was sending more men inland to build more posts and
give the North West Company a run for its money. By
1802, HBC men had reached Athabasca and actually set
up shop right next door to the Nor'Wester depot of
Fort Chipewyan.

But more than the times were changing. Thompson
himself was a different man. Ten years after joining the
North West Company he was married, a father, and a
wintering partner (in modern terms, a member of the
board of directors). Thus he had to take a more
favourable view of trading.

In the summer of 1799, on his way down to Grand
Portage from the Athabasca country, Thompson
stopped off at the Nor'Wester post of Isle-à-la-Crosse
on the upper waters of the Churchill River. At one time
this post had been managed by Patrick Small, a
wintering partner who had been in the pays d'en haut
for about 20 years. Small had retired to England,
leaving behind his Cree wife, a son, and two
daughters, Nancy and Charlotte. Charlotte was now 14
years old, an age at which Indians and Métis were
often married. No portrait of her is known to exist, and
Thompson in his shy way simply describes her as
"lovely." She undoubtedly was, and not only in her
husband's opinion. Alexander Mackenzie, who had a
keen eye for a pretty girl, says that "of all the natives

WEST OF THE MOUNTAINS

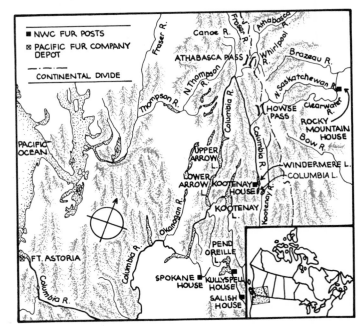

which I have seen on this continent, the Knisteneaux
[Cree] women are the most comely."

Their marriage was an enduring union. Charlotte
went with him on many of his travels, and it was no
uncommon sight to see them, accompanied by several
of their children, in a canoe going up and down the
Saskatchewan or encamped in some deep mountain
valley. Thompson and his wife had seven sons and six
daughters. Unlike most Nor'Westers, Thompson did
not abandon his wife or family when he left the West.
They were parted only by his death 58 years later, and
Charlotte survived him by just three months.

Thompson's promotion to partner came in 1804.
Two years later, he was asked to pioneer a way
through the Rockies and set up a brand-new
department of the Company west of the mountains.

John McDonald of Garth, a senior Nor'Wester
partner and the man in charge of the Fort des Prairies
(Saskatchewan) Department, had Thompson
transferred from the Churchill River Department to his
command. McDonald wanted Thompson to establish
trading posts on the Pacific slope. The fur trade was
reaching farther and farther up the North
Saskatchewan, a series of moves from one thoroughly

exploited beaver region to the next untapped one westward. McDonald was keen to move into the mountains, the next likely source of profits.

McDonald knew Thompson well. They were actually brothers-in-law, McDonald having married Nancy Small. He considered Thompson a good trader, a fearless traveller, and a man who was liked and respected by Indians. Indeed, McDonald's few criticisms of his brother-in-law had to do with his piety, his passion for surveying, and his total unwillingness to drink or to employ liquor when dealing with customers. Thompson had seen so many Indian men and women made foolish — or murderous — by spirits that he had gradually acquired a violent hatred of alcohol and refused to use it as a bribe:

I was obliged to take two kegs of alcohol, overruled by my partners (Messrs Donald McTavish and John McDonald of Garth), for I had made it a law to myself that no alcohol should pass the mountains in my company, and thus be clear of the sad sight of drunkenness and its many evils. But these gentlemen insisted upon alcohol being the most profitable article that could be taken for the Indian trade. . . . When we came to the defiles of the mountains I placed the two kegs of alcohol on a vicious horse, and by noon the kegs were empty and in pieces . . . I wrote to my partners what I had done and that I would do the same to every keg of alcohol, and for the next six years I had charge of the fur trade on the west side of the mountains, no further attempt was made to introduce spirituous liquors.

Thompson was no stranger to the eastern slopes of the mountains. He had examined them five years earlier as a member of an expedition trying to find a pass through the massive, saw-toothed barrier of the Rockies. He had ridden up the Bow River Valley and, somewhere near the modern town of Banff, climbed a mountain to see for himself the difficulties involved. Thompson was stunned by the spectacle of range after range of snow-topped mountains stretching off to the horizon. "Never before did I behold so just, so perfect a resemblance to the waves of the ocean in a wintry storm." Then he tried to find a pass farther north, a pass that Indian reports said was at the headwaters of the North Saskatchewan River. But it was too late in the summer to do this. The many streams feeding the river were swollen with glacial meltwater and far too violent to travel.

Except for perhaps a few wandering Indians and a handful of "freemen," French-Canadian trappers working for themselves, the one person who had managed to get beyond the barrier of the Rocky Mountains was Alexander Mackenzie. And he had only succeeded in 1793 by going up the Peace River, a powerful waterway that had cut its own passage right through the Rockies. But Mackenzie had not found a navigable canoe route to and from the Pacific. The raging waters, boiling rapids, and brutal portages of the mountainous country west of the Rockies had gradually torn his canoe apart. Then it took him two weeks to march through the cold valleys and cloudy plains of the coastal ranges. When Mackenzie finally reached the Pacific, it was in a canoe borrowed from local Indians.

So, in 1806, Thompson had two tasks. First, he had to discover a pass. Then he had to locate navigable waters before building up a fur-trading operation.

Thompson quickly found out there was a third task —to dodge the Piegans. His base of operations, Rocky Mountain House, was in their territory. Taking goods into the mountains, in particular muskets, powder, and ammunition, would not be easy while these Indians kept watch on the fur post. Over the course of many years, they had used guns bought both from the

A fur trader who found a way across the Rocky Mountains found his way barred by range after range of mountains running north and south. What, then, was Alexander Mackenzie's route to the Pacific? How did Simon Fraser get to the Pacific?

Hudson's Bay Company and the Nor'Westers to drive several Indian rivals, notably the Kootenays, west of the mountains. The Piegans did not want to see a balance-of-power situation develop as soon as their enemies, in turn, acquired firearms. So scouts ranged up and down the North Saskatchewan River to turn back any trader's canoes, and warriors visited Rocky Mountain House to drop heavy hints that Thompson should stay right where he was. Nonetheless, he began assembling men, horses, and supplies to cross over the following year. And he ordered "Jaco" Finlay, a half-Indian guide and interpreter, to follow the North Saskatchewan into the mountains and blaze a trail to a river said to be just on the other side of the Rockies.

Then fate lent Thompson a helping hand. In the summer of 1806, part of the famous Lewis and Clark expedition overland to the Pacific was attacked by some Piegans on a horse-raiding expedition. Two warriors were killed by the Americans. After brooding on the incident all winter, several war parties raged south to the upper Missouri in the spring of 1807 to avenge their comrades' deaths on anyone who crossed their paths. The way to the mountains was open.

Thompson set off west with his party, which included his wife and three children, the youngest in a wooden cradle board on her mother's back. They paddled up the North Saskatchewan as far as the Kootenay Plains, a beautiful, broad stretch of grass and woodland. On the next stage west they had to lead pack horses into the mountains through the entrance dominated on the north by the crags of Mount Wilson and on the south by the massive ledges of Mount Murchison. (At this point, Thompson was roughly halfway between the modern towns of Banff and Jasper.) Once through this opening, they followed Finlay's poorly blazed trail up a pleasantly wooded valley containing a wide, placid river (the Howse) until they were in an open, park-like area at the foot of a gap in the mountains. Barely 50 miles north was the cluster of mighty peaks that encircles the greatest body of ice in the Rocky Mountains, the 130-square-mile Columbia Icefield, a relic of the ice ages and the genesis of many glaciers.

"Here among the stupendous and solitary wilds covered with eternal

Many of the Indians of the plateau country in the British Columbia interior spoke in the Salishan, Athapaskan, or Kootenayan languages. How, then, did fur traders, accustomed to the Algonkian, Siouan, or Athapaskan languages, communicate with these plateau people?

snow, and mountain connected with mountain by immense glaciers, the collection of ages and on which the beams of the sun make hardly any impression when aided by the most favourable weather, I stayed fourteen days more, impatiently waiting for the melting of the snows of the height of land."

The height of land is the continental divide that twists and winds its way through the Rocky Mountains and separates waters flowing to the Arctic, to Hudson Bay, and to the Pacific. Where the divide crosses the top of the Howse Valley is what Thompson called "Mountain Portage," a narrow wilderness trail (Howse Pass) leading to the western side of the mountains.

On June 25th, the little party made the stiff climb up to the divide, which is 5,000 feet above sea level here and flanked on the west by the awesome, glistening masses of the Freshfield Icefield. It took them five days to descend the western slope, days spent guiding tired, bad-tempered pack horses alongside a raging torrent (Blaeberry River) that tumbles down through some 40 miles of heavily timbered country before finally levelling out on the broad floor of a huge valley. The Blaeberry enters a larger waterway that Thompson christened the "Kootenae." (At this point he was just a few miles north of the modern town of Golden, British Columbia.) Deceived both by the river's northward flow and its location so far from the Pacific coast—and thus completely unaware that it was the Columbia—Thompson turned south and made his way about 70 miles to a point close to a mountain lake (Windermere, the lower of the two lakes from which the Columbia flows). Here, he had his men build Kootenae House.

Anticipating trouble from the Piegans, Thompson made sure that the post was stockaded on three sides, the fourth being the steep bank of the river. It was just as well he took precautions. A Piegan war party arrived late in the fall, not so much to attack as to hang about and disrupt any trading with the Kootenays. But the Piegan tired of their watch and withdrew, leaving Thompson free to spend the winter doing a lot of profitable business with his new customers.

Thompson concentrated intensely on business matters for the next three years. McDonald of Garth had left the pays d'en haut in 1808 owing to ill health, and the district west of the mountains was formed into the Columbia Department with Thompson in charge. Another powerful motive is clear from a few lines in a letter he sent to Alexander Fraser, a fellow Nor'Wester:

" . . . It is my wish to give all my children an equal and good education; my conscience obliges me to it and it is for this I am now working in this country. . . . If all goes well and it pleases good Providence to take care of me, I hope to see you and a civilized world in the autumn of 1812."

Thompson had been due to "go down in rotation" to Montreal for 12-months' leave in 1808, yet there was no respite for him that year. He was only 38 years old but, like many colleagues of his age, he was discovering that the hardships of the fur trade were better suited to younger men. He wanted to acquire as much money as possible and retire. He also had a long-cherished ambition to produce a map of the western country. Thompson only needed some time west of the mountains to complete the geographical facts he required. He already had Mackenzie's report of his voyage to the Pacific, together with information being sent him by an old friend and fellow partner, Simon Fraser, who was trading farther north in the Company's New Caledonia Department and also seeking the same elusive river: the Columbia.

Simon Fraser and his voyageurs

Between April and December, 1808, Thompson accomplished a fantastic amount of travel, in the course of which he opened up several new trading areas. First of all he and a few of his men set off south down that extraordinary valley we call the Rocky Mountain Trench, an immense trough anywhere from two to ten miles wide that separates the Rockies from the other western ranges. After one day's canoeing from Kootenae House, they portaged a few miles to the source of what Thompson called the "Flat Bow" or "McGillivray's river" (really the Kootenay River), which carried them far down the Trench into what is now United States territory. In the course of following the great turn the river makes back north, they came upon a camp of Kootenays and Flatheads. After extracting a promise from them to trade — which may not have been difficult because they had been attacked with firearms by Piegans a few days earlier — Thompson pushed on briefly downriver to Kootenay Lake (in southeast British Columbia). Returning upriver to the Indians' camp, he bought horses for his party and set off northeast across country until he met up with the Kootenay River again, which led him back to Kootenae House. He had been gone six weeks and had journeyed about 600 miles.

A few days later, loading his family and the winter's take in furs onto horses, he led his party back over the pass above the headwaters of the North Saskatchewan and embarked in a canoe they had left at Kootenay Plains the previous year. Before travelling to Rainy Lake House some 1,500 miles to the east, he left his family at a post some way downriver from Rocky Mountain House. His wife was within a month or two of giving birth to their fourth child. On August 2nd, Thompson reached the Rainy Lake depot and hastily replaced his bales of furs with packs of trade goods. Two days later he hurried off. By October 31st, he and his family (including a new baby boy) were back on the Columbia. Before the year was out, he had dispatched his principal assistant, Finan McDonald, to build a trading post down at the big bend of the Kootenay.

In April 1809, when the winter's trade at Kootenae House was finished, Thompson took out the season's pelts as far as Fort Augustus (near the site of the present city of Edmonton). Here, he arranged the transport of provisions and goods from Rainy Lake House to his mountain base. By August he was back again at the western end of the big bend of the Kootenay River. Obtaining horses from local friends, he rode south to Pend Oreille Lake, where he found a large camp of Flatheads and other Indians. On the east side of the lake, close to the mouth of the Clark Fork River, he built Kullyspell House. In November he followed the Clark Fork upstream, built a second post for the Flathead trade (Salish House), wintering there.

Although working hard to increase Company profits during these years, Thompson did not entirely resist the temptation to do some surveying. He had, of course, tracked what he called the "Kootenae" to its source (Columbia Lake), although he was still unaware that this was really the Columbia River. While based at Kullyspell House several hundred miles south of this valley, he twice canoed westward over Pend Oreille Lake and down the turbulent Pend Oreille River to find out if it could be used as a trade route. But each time its waters proved to be unnavigable, and he had to turn back.

On his second attempt, if Thompson had portaged or marched another 30 miles, he would have come to a large waterway flowing southwest. It would have taken him all the way to the Pacific Ocean. It was the great river of the Pacific Northwest that, first, Alexander Mackenzie, and then Simon Fraser had tried but failed to find: the Columbia.

The southern end of Columbia Lake, British Columbia, the source of the Columbia River; on the right are the Rocky Mountains. On a map, trace the course of the river. Give two reasons why it took David Thompson several years to trace the Columbia's course from the Rocky Mountains to the Pacific Ocean.

Chapter 7 The Columbia

The year 1810 was a most important one in David Thompson's life. In the course of it he experienced both great humiliation and great triumph.

In April that year, Thompson left Finan McDonald in charge at Salish House and set out with numerous packloads of furs on the long haul to Rainy Lake House far to the east. At this time, his wife and family were at a post in the pays d'en haut. Thompson was to be very thankful that they were not with him in 1810.

He and his party managed to reach the Blaeberry River without incident, although on his way up the Rocky Mountain Trench he noted on June 9th:

> . . . the fresh tracks of Piegan scouts. . . . On examining the tracks, found they had gone up the river to recross the mountains . . . a few hours sooner [we] should have had to fight a battle, which thank God is thus avoided.

Once up and over the continental divide, he embarked on the clear, ice-cold waters of the Howse River, deep in the alpine valley fed by the glaciers of the Freshfield Icefield. As always at this time of year, the meltwater from ice and snow made the upper waters of the river a raging torrent. A careful watch had to be kept for sawyers — trees torn from the banks by the current and later grounded by their roots in shallow river stretches. They were just near enough to the surface to rip a birchbark canoe to shreds and leave its occupants at the mercy of rock and rapid.

Natural hazards were not Thompson's only worries. On June 20th, he made camp at the foot of high crags of limestone in case he was attacked by Piegans. He had good reason to be wary. Indians were often unpredictable in the way in which they expressed their anger. The history of the fur trade includes a few incidents where the enmity of customers cost a trader his life when he might well have anticipated only being looted of his goods. As Thompson said of the Piegan, "they were determined to wreak their vengeance on the white men who crossed the mountains to the west side and furnished arms and ammunition to their enemies." In all probability they were out to kill him as a warning to the Company to confine its operations east of the mountains.

There is still confusion about the orders that awaited him when he reached Rainy Lake House. Some Canadian historians think he was instructed to find and survey the Columbia to its mouth as quickly as possible and thus stake a claim to the entire Columbia region before an American rival — John Jacob Astor's Pacific Fur Company — did so by establishing a trading post at the mouth of the river. This theory is convincing but for one thing: it lacks proof that Thompson was ever given such instructions. So what does Thompson himself say about his orders for 1810-11? The *Narrative* contains little or no helpful information. But, from his field journals, there is reason to believe that he considered his instructions were to get to the mouth of the Columbia and oppose Astor's men.

What is much more baffling than the orders Thompson received is his behaviour between late July and the end of October, 1810. The *Narrative* account of this period is barely three pages long, though some curious happenings occurred during these three months. On his way back to the Columbia via the North Saskatchewan, Thompson was out of contact with his canoe brigade for quite some time, although the reasons for this are not made clear. He suggests that there was a fight between his voyageurs and Piegans but fails to describe or explain what happened in this encounter.

Thompson's account of these months is not only suspiciously vague, but a very curious piece of writing. Everywhere else in his *Narrative* he writes in the first person singular. But when recounting his men's trouble with the Piegans, he suddenly switches to the first person plural. "We found them [the voyageurs] at a trading post [Rocky Mountain House] lately deserted." "We fully perceived that we had no further hopes of passing in safety by . . . the Saskatchewan River." "We must now change our route to . . . the Athabaska River." But who were the unexplained "we"? Thompson and his second-in-command, William Henry? Or was Thompson actually referring to

John Jacob Astor, German by birth and upbringing and American by choice, made his fortune largely from land investment and speculation in and around New York City. His attempt to control the fur trade of the Columbia River country from the post of Fort Astoria at the river's mouth failed. Why, then, is he so often recorded in history books as a shrewd fur merchant?

an old trade colleague and friend, Alexander Henry (William Henry's cousin), without mentioning his name?

Alexander Henry the Younger, so called to distinguish him from an uncle of the same name, also a fur trader and merchant, was another North West Company partner. He was in the same area as Thompson at the same time. Henry's job was to revive Rocky Mountain House as a trading centre, and his journals contain a very different, quite detailed account of the whole Piegan episode.

To make a long story short, Henry arrived at Rocky Mountain House to find Thompson's voyageurs there, safe and unharmed, waiting for a leader they said they hadn't seen in twenty days. A friendly Piegan chief had warned them to go back to the post because "four tents" of warriors were waiting farther upstream to ambush them. Thinking quickly, Henry invited these warriors to come to the post for an evening's drinking, got them helplessly drunk, and sent the canoemen upriver towards Howse Pass just before dawn. That same evening, who turned up but his cousin William, to say that Thompson was *downriver* on a tributary called the Brazeau. Here, a day later, Alexander Henry found him "on top of a hill 300 feet above the water, where tall pines stood so thickly that I could not see his tent until we came within ten yards of it." He had been there for the better part of four weeks and was starving, presumably because to fire a gun would attract Piegan attention. According to Henry, he persuaded Thompson to try to cross the mountains by a much more northerly route—an old Indian trail that Henry had heard was somewhere near the headwaters of the Athabasca River. He therefore contacted Thompson's men, supplied them with horses, and redirected them across country to join their leader in the search for this new pass. In this way they avoided the Piegans.

Did Thompson lose his nerve and go into hiding? It was strict Company orders for a partner to be with his canoemen at all times on the march except when hunting buffalo, deer, or game, so where on earth was Thompson for almost a month? What was he doing? Since Henry had got Thompson's men well on the way to Howse Pass, why didn't Thompson circle past

Rocky Mountain House and rejoin them? For that
matter, why was William Henry, the
second-in-command, looking for the canoes?
(Thompson never explains why he, the leader, stayed
where he was.) And why is there absolutely no
mention made of Alexander Henry. Why is no credit
given him for all his help?

What actually happened that fall on the North
Saskatchewan River will probably never be clearly
established. There is no known record with which to
check Alexander Henry's story. But the episode is
strangely like Thompson's account of his expedition to
Lake Athabasca in 1796. In both instances, he doesn't
actually tell any lies. But he doesn't tell the whole story
either. Was he such a proud man that he could never
admit making a mistake? Or did he set himself such
high standards of behaviour and achievement that he
was simply too deeply ashamed of his shortcomings to
confess them?

If Thompson's actions in the September and
October of 1810 are questionable, those for the winter
of 1810-11 are quite clear (and are largely substantiated
by Alexander Henry's journals). He made heroic efforts
to resume and extend the Company's trading
operations on the Pacific slope.

Thompson's many hardships started when he and
his men were forced to spend the better part of four
weeks hacking their way through thick brush and
timber on their northwest course to the Athabasca
River. Movement became much easier when they
emerged onto frozen marshland and swamp near the
river itself. But the intense cold, often as low as 30
degrees below zero, steadily sapped their strength and
made them tired and clumsy much of the time.

What with the bitter weather and the continual
need to hunt to supplement their food supplies, it was
December 30th before they began to follow the broad
valley of the Athabasca into the mountains. At this
point, most of the horses were so exhausted that the
trade goods had to be transported by dog sleds hastily
constructed out of logs. To make matters worse, game
proved scarce. Thompson, still low on provisions and
reduced to slaughtering several horses in order to eke
out food supplies, was forced to send some of his men

back to Rocky Mountain House. About this time a few deserted and returned to the fur post, bluntly telling Alexander Henry that the condition of the men still with Thompson was "pitiful."

The weather remained well below zero as the party slogged on into ever deepening snow, in which the dogs floundered and the sleds stuck time after time. Where the tributary of the Miette joins the Athabasca River (just south of modern Jasper), Thompson had no choice but to lighten the sleds and leave William Henry with the surplus goods. Here, too, he turned loose the few remaining horses. Some of his voyageurs had to shoulder the packs the horses had carried.

Thirteen men and eight dog sleds laboured on south up the wide wooded valley of the Athabasca for about another 15 miles until their Indian guide halted and looked back to the northwest. After checking their position with that of a great peak (Mount Edith Cavell),

The lower valley of the Whirlpool River (Alberta), which led David Thompson past the southeast span of Mount Edith Cavell (left middle ground), past Mount Evans (left foreground), and on up to the Athabasca Pass. Why were rivers, frozen or free-running, the only highways through regions like this?

which in later years came to be called "the Mountain of the Grand Crossing," he pointed the way up a frozen waterway (Whirlpool River) that came from the southwest out of a long mist-shrouded valley.

On January 8th by which date they had trekked painfully but steadily up to the 5,000-foot level through low clouds and swirling snowstorms, Thompson noted what must have been chinook weather:

"We marched ten miles today; and as we advance we feel the mild weather from the Pacific Ocean. This morning at 7 a.m. Ther [mometer] + 6, at 9 p.m. + 22 . . ."

January 9th. Ther +32. SE wind and snowed all day, which made hauling very bad. We could proceed only four miles, this partly up a brook and then over a steep high point with dwarf pines. We had to take only half a load and return for the rest. The snow is full seven feet deep, tho' firm and wet, yet the dogs often sunk in it; but our snowshoes did [not] sink more than three inches; and the weather so mild that the snow is dropping from the trees and everything wet . . .

By the morning of the 10th the temperature had dropped back to 16 degrees, but Thompson and his men were clear of the timber line. He sensed that they were very close to the height of land. That night, a clear and brilliant one, he walked a little way from the campfire and discovered that he was in an immense cut in the mountains and on its western edge. Far below he saw a slender ribbon of ice that wound towards him and then swung around in a big bend and moved away towards the southwest. He guessed — correctly — that this was the Columbia, the river he had long called the "Kootenae."

A day or two later, as his men and the dog sleds stumbled and plunged through the deep snow and dense stands of timber on the steep western slopes of the Rocky Mountains, David Thompson was blazing a trail that many would follow. Largely because of the continual threat of robbery, if not of violence, from Piegans, the crossing he had just made — and, of course, surveyed — became a regular route of the Nor'Westers. After a trail had been cleared through the timber on either side of the pass, traders and supplies poured through it and down the Wood River to the embarkation point at the big, hairpin bend of the Columbia that became known as Canoe Encampment. From here they made their way southeast into Kootenay or Salish country or southwest through what is now southern British Columbia and into the state of Washington. All of this was the great "Inland Empire," the last frontier of the fur trade. The Nor'Westers were to haul a great fortune in furs over the pass.

Chapter 8 "The greatest land geographer who ever lived"

Standing in the desolate, windswept Athabasca Pass and gazing down on that ribbon of ice glistening in the moonlight, Thompson must have felt a tremendous sense of triumph. He had found the river Fraser had sought in vain, the navigable waterway to the Pacific that Mackenzie had dreamed of discovering. He had discovered the Pacific Coast equivalent of the Saskatchewan, the great highway of the prairies.

Thompson's discovery was a fitting climax to 24 years of travel and exploration. And it signalled the end of a long chapter in his life. Little more than a year later he left the West, never to return.

Between January, 1811, when he first set foot in the pass, and May, 1812, when he crossed it to journey to Fort William and report personally to his fellow partners, Thompson had many difficulties to overcome. He was delayed by the steady desertion of men worn out by the cold and their labours or panic-stricken by the silence and vague menace of the snow-clad mountains through which he led them. It was months before he could travel the Columbia in a canoe painfully constructed out of the only materials to hand—cedarwood and pine roots. He had to set off, not downstream, but upriver and along the Kootenay River to the Salish country, where he could pick up fresh men and supplies. From here, he cut across country to reach the Columbia and canoed all the way to its mouth. Then he travelled 1,000 miles back up the Columbia, stopping many times to make friends with local Indians. If he didn't, their trade would be picked up by men sent out from the American fur post of Astoria at the river's mouth.

A painstaking sales manager, Thompson made a

hasty trip through the Athabasca Pass to pick up the goods he had left with William Henry on the Miette River. Hurrying southeastward, he made his way back into the Salish country to a fur post that had fallen into disuse, which he repaired. Early in 1812 he got word that reinforcements of men and fresh supplies of goods had come over the pass. At last, he could hand over his responsibilities and return east to enjoy a long overdue rest—and to rejoin his family.

The winter of 1811-12 had been a good trading season, and Thompson's party travelled with 122 ninety-pound packs of furs. Thus he initiated in person the trade route up the Columbia and over the Athabasca Pass. Several weeks later, picking up his family en route, he arrived at Fort William in mid-summer.

He received a very warm welcome from his fellow partners. According to Company regulations, in order to continue to enjoy his full share of the annual profits, a partner had either to winter in the interior or retire for one year in rotation. Despite this rule, Thompson's notoriously thrifty colleagues voted him his full share of the profits for *three* years, plus £100 expenses, so that he could "finish his charts, maps, etc." at his leisure. This was ample evidence of the high regard in which they held him and how much they appreciated his business efforts and his explorations in the course of 15 years of service.

Thompson settled in Terrebonne near Montreal. Here he achieved his ambition to chart western North America by producing his huge "MAP OF THE NORTH-WEST TERRITORY." Almost as large as one wall of a modern living room, it showed the principal rivers, lakes, portages, mountain peaks, and passes between Hudson Bay and the Pacific Ocean, and from the Great Lakes and the Columbia River in the south to Lake Athabasca in the north. Also marked on the map were the locations of the 74 existing Company posts.

In 1784 (the year Thompson arrived at York Factory), when the great map of the world accompanying the account of Captain James Cook's third voyage was published, almost the whole of the North American continent north and west of Lake Winnipeg appeared as a complete blank. With the

Long after David Thompson left the West, in the Columbia Department of the North West Company "brigades" of pack animals journeyed up and down southern British Columbia every spring and fall. They travelled between Alexandria on the Fraser River and Kamloops on the Thompson River to the Okanagan Valley, and thence by boat to and from the mouth of the Columbia, bringing in goods and taking out furs. What were the distances between Alexandria and Kamloops and the Columbia's mouth? Was this method better than hauling goods and furs between Montreal and the British Columbia interior? Why?

exception of the extreme north and northwestern reaches of the continent, Thompson filled in this immense blank in the course of some 50,000 miles of travel by canoe, on horseback, and on foot. With the possible exception of the *Narrative,* the map is his greatest achievement. It hung in the great hall of Fort William until 1821, when the North West Company was absorbed into the Hudson's Bay Company. Then the map vanished, to turn up again in government archives as inexplicably as it had disappeared from the depot on Lake Superior.

For some time, everything seemed to go well with David Thompson. In the years 1816-26, he achieved recognition as "Astronomer and Surveyor to the British Boundary Commission." On behalf of the British government, he surveyed and mapped the Canada-United States boundary from Lower Canada (Quebec) to the northwest angle of the Lake of the Woods, today the junction of the borders of Ontario, Manitoba, and Minnesota. He left Terrebonne and settled in Williamstown, Glengarry County, Upper Canada (Ontario), where he bought a large house and about 80 acres of land.

A shy, reticent man, Thompson was not much of a socializer. But he never refused an invitation to the homes of several fellow Nor'Westers who had also retired to Glengarry County. And when he was asked by William McGillivray, the managing director of the North West Company, to one of his lavish dinner parties in McGillivray's Montreal mansion, Thompson knew he'd always get a particularly friendly welcome. It was at one such party that Dr. J. J. Bigsby, a fellow member of the Boundary Commission, first knew the pleasure of Thompson's company:

"I was well placed at the table between the Miss McGillivrays and a singular-looking person of about fifty. He was plainly dressed, quiet and observant. His figure was short and compact, and his black hair was worn long all round and cut square, as if by one stroke of the shears, just above the eyebrows. His complexion was of the gardener's ruddy brown, while the expression of his deeply furrowed features was friendly and intelligent. . . . His speech betrayed the Welshman—he has a very powerful mind, and a singular faculty of picture-making. He can create a wilderness and people it with warring savages, or climb the Rocky Mountains with you in a snowstorm, so clearly and palpably, that only shut your eyes and you hear the crack of the rifle, or feel the snowflakes melt on your cheeks as he talks."

These were good years. But they came to an end when the Commission finished its work and Thompson discovered about the same time that his only other source of income had dried up. The North West Company, now part of a reorganized and greatly expanded Hudson's Bay Company, went bankrupt. A further financial difficulty arose from the behaviour of several of his sons. Thompson had set them up in business with his own money. But their ventures failed, and he was obliged to pay off all their debts. Even money he made in the 1830s surveying for government agencies or for private companies in the Muskoka region of Upper Canada, in the eastern townships of Lower Canada, and in Montreal itself could not make up for these considerable losses. He was even forced to sell his Williamstown property.

Some time in the 1840s Thompson began to write the *Narrative* in order to support himself and his wife on whatever he could get for it. He hoped to receive $30 a month as a subsidy from "a few gentlemen" who would "form a Company" and "be entitled to and shall have half the net profits of the publication." But he was no good at promoting himself as an author. Despite the care he took with his writing — and much of the *Narrative* was written at least twice — it was neither subsidized nor printed in his lifetime.

Thompson suffered intermittent attacks of glaucoma and was actually blind at various times throughout the last nine years of his life. During that period he and his wife were totally dependent upon the charity of a son-in-law. Despite this, he was obliged to sell some of his clothing and his precious instruments to procure money for food. David Thompson died early in 1857 in circumstances of extreme poverty. He was buried in Mount Royal Cemetery, Montreal.

Obscurity surrounded Thompson even after death. For some strange reason, the wilderness trail by which he had first found a way to the Columbia was called Howse Pass after an HBC trader of Thompson's day. The gap in the ice-encased heights where he made his magnificent crossing in 1811 remains known to this day as the Athabasca Pass. (The Thompson Pass in the Canadian Rockies is named for C.S. Thompson, the alpinist, who crossed over here in 1900). While he was still an HBC man, his notebooks and maps were passed by the Company to Aron Arrowsmith, the first of a famous family of cartographers in London. He incorporated their information in his maps of British North America, information for which the Hudson's Bay Company was credited. Similarly, Arrowsmith's revisions of his map of North America first published in 1795 were based on details of Thompson's work passed on to him by the North West Company. Again, no acknowledgement of Thompson was ever made.

The fur trade declined, and settlers moved into the Pacific Northwest, but Thompson had no mention in early histories of the region. Only a secondary river winding its way through the interior of British Columbia bore his name. Few people knew why it was called the Thompson. Yet it was Simon Fraser who had named it as a mark of his respect for the colleague who had explored the headwaters of the Mississippi.

David Thompson might have remained a mere footnote to history had it not been for the curiosity of a Canadian who was himself something of an explorer.

During the early 1880s, Joseph Burr Tyrrell was working in the Rocky Mountains as field geologist and assistant to the chief of the Geological Survey of Canada. Tyrrell became extremely impressed by the general accuracy of the government maps of the West issued to him. When he tried to find out who had drawn them, he was puzzled to learn that nobody knew. Tyrrell spent several years investigating the mystery. Finally, a few reference notes in an American historian's multi-volume study of the North Pacific coast led Tyrrell to the Crown Lands Department of the Province of Ontario in Toronto. Here, he found a dusty collection of 39 journals, 11 books of field notes, and a large yellowing map of the western half of North America between the 45th and 60th parallels.

After he had studied the journals and found them to be Thompson's, Tyrrell published *A Brief Narrative of the Journeys of David Thompson in North-Western America.* Some time later, he was approached by the Registrar of Deeds for Toronto, who explained that one of Thompson's sons had sold him the manuscript of his father's *Narrative.* Some years later Tyrrell purchased the manuscript and edited and published it.

Tyrrell's high opinion of David Thompson as an explorer and geographer is not hard to understand. The man had earned his living primarily as a fur trader. Yet, in the course of 28 years in western North America, he managed to survey, plot, and map almost two *million* square miles of terrain. He accomplished all this by such extensive travel and observation that, as late as 1915, many maps issued by the Canadian government, by railway companies, and other agencies were based on the cartographic work done by Thompson over a hundred years before.

Tyrrell often said that David Thompson was "the greatest land geographer who ever lived." No one has ever bettered this description.

The title of David Thompson's great map, which can be seen today in the Archives of Ontario, Grenville Street, Toronto. Describe the personalities mentioned. (The modern historical spelling of "John Stewart" is John Stuart.)

This Map made for the North West Company in 1813 and 1814 and delivered to The Honorable William Mc Gillivray then agent Embraces the Region lying between 45 and 60 degrees North Latitude and 84 and 124 degrees West Longitude comprising the Surveys and Discoveries of 20 years namely The Discovery and Survey of the Oregon Territory to the Pacific Ocean the survey of the Athabasca Lake, Slave River and Lake from which flows Mackenzies River to the Arctic Sea by Mr Philip Turner the Route of Sir Alexander Mackenzie in 1792 down part of Frasers River

together with the Survey of this River to the
Pacific Ocean by the late John Stewart
of the North West Company
by David Thompson
Astronomer and Surveyor

David Thompson

Further Reading

The best source of information on David Thompson is, of course, David Thompson. But Tyrrell's edition of the *Narrative* (1916) is not recommended. It is hard to obtain and it is biased: Tyrrell presents Thompson as a man more or less without faults. Instead, read *David Thompson's Narrative 1784-1812*, edited with an introduction and notes by Richard Glover and published in 1962 by the Champlain Society. This edition contains a critical introduction to Thompson and his times; in addition, Glover has retained Tyrrell's year-by-year itinerary of Thompson's travels and many footnotes in the 1916 edition that are vital to understanding Thompson and his achievements.

A more readily available book is Victor G. Hopwood's *David Thompson, Travels in Western North America, 1784-1812*, Macmillan of Canada, 1971. Although a condensed version of the *Narrative*, this is a valuable guide to Thompson's achievements as explorer, geographer, and author.

The Canadian Rockies, Early Travels and Explorations, E. Fraser. Edmonton: M.G. Hurtig Ltd., 1969.

The Course of Empire, B. DeVoto. Boston: Houghton, Mifflin, 1952.

The Explorers of North America, 1492-1806, T.B. Brebner. New York: Doubleday, 1955.

Fur Trade, Rosemary Neering, Toronto: Fitzhenry & Whiteside, 1974.

The Fur Trade and the Northwest to 1857, E.E. Rich. Toronto: McClelland & Stewart, 1967.

Fur Trade Canoe Routes of Canada/Then and Now, E.W. Morse. Ottawa: Queen's Printer, 1969.

Fur Trade in Canada, rev. ed., H. Innes. Toronto: University of Toronto Press, 1956.

The North West Company, M.W. Campbell. Toronto: Macmillan, 1973.

The Pedlars from Quebec, and Other Papers on the Nor'Westers, W.S. Wallace. Toronto: The Ryerson Press, 1954.

Credits

The publishers wish to express their gratitude to the following who have given permission to use copyrighted illustrations in this book:

Provincial Archives of Alberta, page 49.
Archives of Ontario, page 37.
British Columbia Government, page 44.
Centennial Museum, Vancouver, B.C., page 17.
The Champlain Society, pages 38,61.
Hudson's Bay Company, Winnipeg, page 35.
Information Canada, pages 8,9,18.
Minnesota Historical Society, page 27.
The National Gallery of Canada, page 39.
National Maritime Museum, Greenwich, England, pages 32,33.
New York Public Library, page 51.
Parks Canada, pages 3,5,18.
Public Archives of Canada, pages 39,47.
United States National Park Service, page 25.

Editing: Laura Damania
Design: Jack Steiner
Cover Illustration: Steven Pilcher

The Canadians

Consulting Editor: Roderick Stewart
Editor-in-Chief: Robert Read

Every effort has been made to credit all sources correctly. The author and publishers will welcome any information that will allow them to correct any errors or omissions.

Índice

Conocer al Golden Retriever

Quienquiera que haya dicho: «no puedes tenerlo todo», no conoce al Golden Retriever.

El Golden Retriever es uno de los perros de compañía más populares del mundo, pero es también muy utilizado por los cazadores debido a su gran talento para el cobro.

De brillante cobrador de aves acuáticas a comienzos del siglo XX, el Golden se ha metamorfoseado en un perro que hace de todo y se destaca en cualquier servicio canino. El Golden Retriever de nuestros días guía ciegos, asiste a minusválidos, detecta drogas y explosivos, localiza personas sepultadas en los escombros como consecuencia de terremotos y otros desastres, y consuela a jóvenes y ancianos en hospitales y sanatorios. Eso sin olvidar su papel más importante: ser el mejor amigo y, a veces, el compañero de caza, de su familia humana. Por eso no resulta extraño contemplar por doquier –desde las tarjetas de felicitación hasta las cajas de cereales y los suéteres– el rostro sonriente del Golden Retriever.

Con toda seguridad, el hombre que dio origen al primer Golden no tenía noción alguna del valor del imperio que estaba fundando. El primer lord Tweedmouth de Guisachan (antes sir Dudley Marjoriebanks) sólo soñaba con un cobrador amarillo mejor que los existentes, capaz de cobrar los patos abatidos en las heladas aguas del río Tweed, cerca de la costa escocesa. Con ese fin, en 1868, Tweedmouth inició un ambicioso programa de cría cruzando a Nous, su Wavy-Coated Retriever (Cobrador de Pelo Rizado) de color amarillo, (proveniente de una camada de cachorros completamente negros, antepasados del actual Flat Coated Retriever) con una Tweed Water Spaniel llamada Belle. El Tweed Water Spaniel era un apreciado perro de caza, conocido por su inteligencia, excepcionales habilidades natatorias y dócil temperamento. Aquel apareamiento produjo cuatro cachorros peludos que se convirtieron en los antepasados del versátil Golden Retriever que hoy conocemos.

Tweedmouth se quedó con un cachorro amarillo al que apodó Cowslip, y dio los otros tres a algunos amigos que compartían

¿Cuando piensa en el Golden le viene a la mente el lobo? Puede que no, pero es el antecesor común de todos los perros.

El Golden ama el agua, por eso es un nadador natural. Cobrando es tan bueno en el agua como en tierra. Su pelaje impermeable le permite trabajar bajo cualquier tipo de condiciones climáticas.

con él su sueño «dorado». El programa reproductor de Tweedmouth se concentraba en «fijar» el gen productor del amarillo en un cobrador amante del agua y con un temperamento fuera de serie. La progenie, resultado de esos cruzamientos y de los de sus asociados, continuó produciendo perros de caza del tipo Golden, muy apreciados por su gran coraje, sagacidad y temperamento. Los historiadores de entonces también se refirieron a la especial habilidad de la raza para vincularse con las personas: «Rivaliza con todas las otras razas por el apego que tiene con su amo», descripción que se ajusta perfectamente a nuestro moderno Golden Retriever.

Los Golden Retrievers fueron registrados por primera vez en la Sociedad Canina Inglesa *(The Kennel Club)* en 1903, dentro de la categoría general de Retrievers (cobradores). En 1913 fueron reconocidos como «Yellow o Golden Retrievers»; el término *yellow* (amarillo) dejó de utilizarse en 1920.

La raza llegó a los Estados Unidos a principios del siglo XX y obtuvo el reconocimiento oficial de la Sociedad Canina Estadounidense *(American Kennel Club,* AKC) en 1925. Los primeros Golden se destacaron como perros de caza poderosos y valientes, capaces de trabajar duro y a la vez competir en las exposiciones caninas. La separación distintiva entre el perro de caza y el de exposición no ocurrió hasta que la raza remontó la ola de la popularidad en la década de 1950.

Gracias a la pasión que sentía Tweedmouth por un cobrador inteligente y dócil, el Golden del siglo XXI ha conservado muchas de las cualidades que más valoraba su creador. Aunque la mayoría de los Golden de hoy pasan más tiempo deambulando por la casa que cazando patos, todavía se considera que son los perros más aptos para ir de cacería, participar en competencias, o simplemente convivir con ellos y colmarlos de abrazos.

El Golden Retriever actual se destaca indiscutiblemente por su «abrazabilidad». Para esta raza no existen los extraños y por eso saluda a todas las personas con el mismo entusiasmo que a sus viejos amigos. Tal afabilidad hace del Golden el candidato ideal para el trabajo de terapia en hospitales y sanatorios.

Como lazarillo y perro asistente, el Golden no tiene igual. Su habilidad para ligarse con su camarada humano es legendaria. En el trabajo de búsqueda y rescate ha trabajado valientemente durante muchos desastres, especialmente durante la tragedia del 11 de septiembre de 2001, demostrando que todavía tiene el coraje de sus antepasados.

En el campo, muchos Golden todavía demuestran su valor como perros de cacería. Constantemente ratifican su brillante olfato en la caza de montaña y en el cobro de aves acuáticas bajo temperaturas inferiores a cero grado. También se destacan en las pruebas y competencias de caza, y en las muy exigentes competencias de campo.

Pocas razas superan al Golden en su gusto por la vida. Es un perro que disfruta cada momento del día, que explora cada agujero y cada rincón del patio con el mismo entusiasmo de Colón cuando descubrió América,

y que le encanta cobrar estacas y palos el doble de su tamaño.

Se le conoce como perro muy «bucal» ya que le encanta tomar con la boca brazos y manos de puro entusiasmo. Encuentra y devuelve todo lo que está a su alcance, especialmente

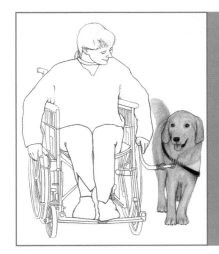

El talento del Golden ha trascendido el campo a medida que se le ha usado en muchas áreas del servicio canino. Como perro asistente, el Golden es un compañero leal y auxiliador que lleva a cabo diferentes tareas para su minusválido dueño.

medias y otras prendas de vestir. Si no se le supervisa, las hará trizas. Los dueños conscientes aprenden rápidamente a mantener todo lejos del suelo mientras esperan que sus Golden maduren (¡no confíe mucho en ello!).

La hermosura del glorioso pelaje del Golden Retriever es

una bendición dudosa, porque es un perro que muda cantidad de pelusas perrunas dos veces al año. Los dueños de Golden dedican gran cantidad de tiempo cada semana a acicalar a sus perros, cepillándoles el dorado y grueso pelaje, y pasando la aspiradora por los muebles. Las personas quisquillosas deberían considerar tener otras razas.

Como perro de trabajo y atleta natural, el Golden necesita ejercicio fuerte. Si no se le da, encaminará su energía a hacer cosas «divertidas» como cavar en el jardín o renovar el mobiliario. Por su alta sociabilidad no es un perro de patio, que pueda vivir separado de su familia.

Se considera que el Golden Retriever es una raza de tamaño entre mediano y grande; los machos miden entre 55 y 60 cm a la cruz, y pesan entre 30 y 35 kg; las hembras miden entre 53 y 57 cm, y pesan entre 25 y 30 kg.

Durante los últimos 20 años, el Golden Retriever se ha mantenido inalterablemente dentro de las cinco razas más registradas en el AKC y la FCI. Pero, lamentablemente, la popularidad tiene un precio. Al igual que ocurre con todas las razas que llaman la atención del público, el Golden moderno es una víctima lastimosa del mercado masivo y de los «criadores de trascorral» productores de Golden en grandes cantidades. Se trata de perros de mala calidad, irritables y enfermizos, agresivos con los demás perros y a veces con la gente. No hay que decir que esta clase de criadores produce Golden Retrievers carentes del deseo básico de cobrar. En otro marco de referencia, los criadores «de especialidades», en su esfuerzo por producir perros que se destaquen en el trabajo de campo, en Obediencia o en conformación, han sacrificado la polifacética índole natural del Golden en función de conseguir perros ganadores dentro de la especialidad para la cual fueron criados.

Dos marcas de fábrica del Golden Retriever: su bellísimo y ondulante pelaje dorado y su fijación bucal. Como cobrador, el Golden difícilmente deja de tener algo en la boca, así que los dueños han de tomar muchas precauciones en este sentido.

Una vez dicho esto, queda claro que la selección del criador reviste gran importancia a la hora de comprar un cachorro de Golden. Los compradores de cachorros deben evitar a todos esos criadores que producen Golden atípicos y enfermizos. De no hacerlo, correrán el riesgo de enfrentar una serie de problemas de salud como la displasia de cadera y de codo (que no sólo conducen a la artritis prematura y la cojera, sino que implicarán grandes gastos veterinarios), las alergias y los problemas de tiroides (más jugosas cuentas veterinarias), o problemas de temperamento como la agresión y la hiperactividad, que pueden desembocar en comportamientos peligrosos o destructivos.

CONOCER AL GOLDEN RETRIEVER

Resumen

■ El Golden Retriever es famoso por ser un perro polifacético: de compañía, de competencia, de caza o de servicio.

■ Lord Tweedmouth, el creador de la raza, intentaba producir un cobrador acuático talentoso capaz de trabajar en medio de las heladas.

■ El programa de cría original fijó muchas características deseables en el Golden, incluyendo la belleza, las habilidades cinegéticas, la inteligencia, la versatilidad, un temperamento maravilloso y una lealtad inigualable.

■ El «cobrador amarillo» de lord Tweedmouth que ha llegado a nuestros días es una de las razas más populares del mundo. Lamentablemente, esa popularidad ha desembocado en la crianza masiva; además, se han producido diferencias en el tipo, según se trate de perros de exposición o de trabajo. Los dueños deberían buscar Golden típicos y correctos, producidos por criadores serios.

Estándar y
descripción de la raza

El estándar oficial de cada raza canina describe detalladamente las diversas cualidades que la diferencian de las demás en conformación, habilidades y carácter.

El del Golden Retriever establece la guía que utilizan los jueces para evaluar a los ejemplares de esta raza, y también los criadores para planificar sus programas de cría. Partiendo de este «modelo» los criadores se esfuerzan por producir auténticos especímenes de la raza. Sin el estándar, el Golden Retriever podría perder con el tiempo todas aquellas cualidades que hacen de él un perro «de oro».

El Golden fue originalmente desarrollado como perro de caza. El estándar racial, en su primer párrafo, *apariencia general,* recalca ese propósito y enfatiza la importancia del Golden como cobrador: «Es un perro activo, simétrico, poderoso y bien armado, no desmañado ni largo de patas, de expresión noble y

La naturaleza del Golden se refleja en esa expresión tan suya: «noble», pero mostrando a la vez una personalidad vehemente, alerta y confiada en sí mismo.

personalidad vehemente, alerta y confiado en sí mismo. Por haber sido concebido originalmente como perro de caza debe exhibírsele en condiciones de trabajo duro, y se debe conferir más importancia a su apariencia general, armonía, marcha y utilidad, que a cualquiera de sus partes componentes.»

Incluso los Golden Retrievers que no cazan (en la actualidad, la mayoría) deben conservar el instinto de caza y atenerse al estándar en cuanto a ser atléticos, musculosos, y estar en condiciones físicas de laboriosa faena. El Golden es un perro que debe estar bien construido para poder participar en actividades deportivas que demanden un alto gasto de energía, ya sea competitivas o el simple juego en el patio persiguiendo una pelota.

En la caracterización integral del Golden son importantes la talla y la proporción. Los machos deben medir entre 55 y 60 cm a la cruz, y las hembras entre 53 y 57. Su longitud, desde el esternón hasta la punta de la nalga, es ligeramente superior

El Golden es una belleza natural, pero su pelaje es sobre todo funcional. Su manto doble e impermeable es el aislante y protector ideal para el trabajo en el agua y en el campo.

He aquí un Golden de primera, acicalado completamente para exposición. Los verdaderos fanáticos del Golden se esmeran en producir perros multipropósito, cuya armonía en cuanto a forma, función y temperamento les permita triunfar en el trabajo, la exposición y el hogar.

a la altura a la cruz en una proporción de 12:11. El peso ideal oscila entre los 30 y 55 kg para los machos, y entre los 25 y las 30 kg para las hembras.

Hoy día se pueden ver Golden bastante más altos de lo que indica el estándar y/o con un peso que puede exceder los 42 kg. Tales perros no son representativos de esta raza, que es de trabajo, y no deben criarse. Un cobrador con mala estructura no será capaz de pasar un día entero cobrando y transportando aves acuáticas y otras presas en tierra firme.

La cabeza y expresión clásicas del Golden Retriever son sus valiosas marcas de fábrica. Los ojos reflejan su alma… «de expresión amistosa e inteligente». En la sección del temperamento, se repite que el Golden es: «Amistoso, confiable y seguro. La pugnacidad u hostilidad hacia otros perros o hacia la gente, en situaciones normales, y la timidez o nerviosismo injustificados, no tienen que ver con el carácter del Golden Retriever.»

El pelaje del Golden es tan funcional como «abrazable», y le sirve de protección tanto contra el calor como contra el frío además de resguardarle de la maleza potencialmente dañina cuando está de caza en tierras altas. Aunque los colores extremos son indeseables, el pelaje del Golden va desde el rojo oscuro hasta el rubio muy pálido. El color del manto es sólo un asunto de preferencia personal.

La típica afabilidad amorosa del Golden hacia todas las personas es quizás la cualidad más definitoria de la raza. Así era el perro amarillo original que cazaba junto a lord Tweedmouth. Los Golden caprichosos o imprevisiblemente hostiles no son típicos de la raza, por lo que deben excluirse de cualquier programa de cría y ser desestimados por los compradores de cachorros.

Claro que el Golden Retriever perfecto o ideal es ciertamente un mito. Y a causa de la divergencia entre las líneas de exposición, trabajo y Obediencia, hay muchos Golden en la actualidad que no son siquiera típicos. Más bien son «especialistas», perros criados en función de la pasión o enfoque particular de un criador determinado. Los perros de trabajo se crían con las cualidades que realzan su comportamiento en el campo y con menos preocupación por algunos de los caracteres físicos emblemáticos del Golden. Los criadores de perros de exposición se concentran en aquellos rasgos que se convertirán en cintas azules en la pista de exposición, y hacen poco o ningún énfasis en su habilidad como perros de caza.

Los competidores de Obediencia crían perros que responden mejor a esa, su pasión personal. Son pocos los que se encuentran entre los extremos y satisfacen las prioridades de todas las especialidades.

Afortunadamente, la mayoría de los Golden de hoy son todavía destacados perros multipropósito. Su amor por la gente, y las diversas funciones que cumplen son herencia de los perros que lord Tweedmouth tanto apreciaba.

ESTÁNDAR Y DESCRIPCIÓN DE LA RAZA

Resumen

■ Todos los Golden deben ser atléticos, musculosos y estar bien construidos, deben ser capaces de pasar un día completo en duras faenas campestres, ya sea que se les use o no para la cacería.

■ El temperamento del Golden es la marca de fábrica de la raza. Se trata de un perro amistoso, sociable y amoroso, por lo que en él resultan muy atípicas la agresión y la timidez, que constituyen faltas graves.

■ El precioso manto del Golden no es sólo bello sino también protector, y sus matices van desde el rubio pálido hasta el oro-rojizo intenso.

■ El Golden típico es armonioso, tal como lo concibió lord Tweedmouth, no el producto de los caprichos y preferencias de un criador.

¿Es la raza adecuada para usted?

Si está acariciando sueños «dorados» debería dar un paso atrás y, antes de lanzarse a localizar un cachorro, decidir qué clase de perro es el que está buscando.

El hecho de que los Golden Retriever sean perros multipropósito, que hacen de todo, no significa que sean adecuados para todos los cinófilos. Parte del misterio del Golden Retriever radica en que no hay dos Golden iguales. Como es natural, cada perro tiene su propia personalidad, pero en una raza tan versátil como el Golden, uno puede encontrar ejemplares con diferencias extremas en cuanto a habilidades y personalidad.

Al margen de esto, todos los Golden son, o deberían ser, perros que aman a la gente, que saludan lo mismo al amigo que al extraño como si fueran viejos socios que hace siglos no ven. Viven mejor dentro de la casa, en compañía de la familia, y no prosperan si se les aísla de los humanos a

Siendo un auténtico perro familiar, al Golden Retriever le encanta acurrucarse con la gente que ama, o sea, ¡con todo el mundo!

quienes tanto aman. Al contrario de lo que algunas imágenes de Golden típicos parecen decir, son perros de trabajo altamente energéticos que necesitan mucha atención y ejercicio diario. Disfrutan las diversiones y juegos activos al aire libre, opciones excelentes para dar salida a su entusiasmo y energía. ¿Está seguro de que su disposición personal y estilo de vida son compatibles con las necesidades de este perro?

Un juguete para mordisquear, agua para chapotear y miembros de la familia dedicándole tiempo: ¿qué más puede necesitar un Golden?

El Golden tiene fama de ser una criatura bucal porque adora llevar algo… cualquier cosa… en la boca, y eso incluye su mano, brazo, medias, y cualquier otro objeto que no esté bien clavado. Pleno de felicidad, «cobrará» sus calzones deportivos para llevárselos al párroco, de visita en casa. Sólo muchos meses de entrenamiento podrán orientar ese instinto bucal hacia una conducta más apropiada.

El mordisqueo es el subproducto natural del cobro, por eso los cachorros de Golden son diminutas máquinas de morder. Muchos arrastran la costumbre a la madurez, dejando evidentes cicatrices en el mobiliario y la

Un Golden inactivo encontrará algo que hacer. Dejar que un perro activo se aburra es ¡buscarse problemas!

marquetería. El dueño inteligente podrá minimizar el daño supervisando diligentemente a su perro, proporcionándole los juguetes de morder adecuados y enseñando al cachorro de Golden lo que puede y lo que no puede mordisquear.

Aquellos dueños que no preparen la casa eliminando de ella todos los riesgos, o que no supervisen a sus cachorros, le contarán terribles anécdotas de las cosas imposibles que sus Golden se han comido o han destruido. Si no está dispuesto a adiestrar a su cachorro o a supervisarlo, prepárese para afrontar las consecuencias.

Los Golden Retrievers son magníficos con los niños pero, por su carácter efusivo, se les debe supervisar a ambos cuando están juntos para evitar cualquier accidente como consecuencia del normal alboroto del Golden.

¿Le sacará de quicio encontrar pelo de perro en su traje o sofá? El vellón encantador del cachorro de Golden se transformará en un largo pelaje espeso que es necesario cepillar frecuentemente para mantenerlo limpio y para evitar que los pelos sueltos terminen en su plato de comida. Los Golden sueltan su pesado pelaje interno en primavera y otoño, pero a lo largo de todo el año mudan un poquito todos los días. Sólo el cepillado regular podrá reducir al mínimo el pelo dentro de la casa. Y no olvide esas patas embarradas que, después de corretear por el jardín, irrumpen en el suelo de la cocina. Son muy pocas las casas con Golden que conservan sus suelos inmaculados.

Los dueños potenciales de Golden deben considerar sus preferencias y necesidades antes de seleccionar al perro y al criador. La separación entre las líneas de campo, exposición y Obediencia ha creado Golden con marcadas diferencias en cuanto a temperamento, habilidad cinegética y estructura. El Golden de campo, criado para cazar, es por lo general más magro y menos peludo, su cabeza suele ser más estrecha, y su nivel de energía, más elevado. El que se cría para conquistar las cintas azules en la pista de exposición es típicamente más pesado de hueso, más cor-

Los dueños de Golden deben estar preparados para el entusiasmo de un perro que adora estar cerca de la gente que ama.

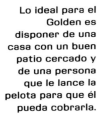

to de patas y con un cráneo notoriamente más ancho. El Golden de exposición es por lo general más sosegado, y menos intenso –si llegara a serlo– en el campo.

No obstante, un cachorro Golden de exposición puede ser todo un reto. Su entusiasmo y gusto por la vida pueden agobiar fácilmente al dueño novel que no está preparado para el vigor y vitalidad naturales de la

placer a la persona que lo entrena, pero necesita aprender cómo hacerlo. El entrenamiento en Obediencia es el camino sensato para transformar al efusivo Golden en un buen y educado ciudadano canino.

Los grupos de socorro de los Golden (organizaciones que buscan nuevos hogares a los Golden abandonados) lidian todos los días con dueños desilusionados que renuncian a sus Golden por

Lo ideal para el Golden es disponer de una casa con un buen patio cercado y de una persona que le lance la pelota para que él pueda cobrarla.

raza. Quizás debido a que es un perro muy conocido, mucha gente no es consciente de que, aun siendo muy adiestrable, el Golden necesita entrenamiento. Está más que ansioso por complacer a la persona que lo entre-

problemas de temperamento o de conducta. El asunto es simple: se trata de perros que nunca fueron adiestrados o, cuando más, lo fueron muy pobremente. Afortunadamente, hay muchos dueños de corazón firme que, aunque han fallado no sometiendo a sus Golden a entrenamiento, aprenden a tolerarlos y, por amor, se adaptan a sus modales revoltosos. Es muy probable que uno de tales perros viva ¡al doblar la esquina!

La selección de la raza y del criador son decisiones de peso que deben basarse en lo que es mejor para usted y para su futuro perro. Todo eso y más deberá

¿Qué el agua no corre? ¡Qué más da! Para el Golden, una zambullida en la piscina familiar es tan buena como nadar en un lago

determinar si usted y un Golden Retriever podrán vivir felizmente juntos.

¿ES LA RAZA ADECUADA PARA USTED?

Resumen

■ El dueño adecuado para el Golden es aquel que disfruta teniendo un perro versátil y talentoso capaz de participar con él y toda su familia en cualquier actividad.

■ El dueño adecuado para el Golden desea hacer de él un verdadero miembro de la familia porque este perro de amoroso temperamento y devoto de los suyos, prospera en compañía de su manada humana.

■ El dueño adecuado para el Golden puede habérselas con un perro altamente energético con las inclinaciones bucales de todo cobrador.

■ El dueño adecuado para el Golden dedicará tiempo al acicalado de su perro durante todo el año, pero aún más durante la primavera y el otoño que son las estaciones de muda.

■ El dueño adecuado para el Golden sabe que para dirigir los talentos y energía de su perro hacia la buena conducta y las ocupaciones positivas, es necesario el entrenamiento.

Selección
del criador

Encontrar una camada de Golden no debe ser difícil, pues parece que hay por lo menos un perro de esta raza en cada perrera.

Sin embargo, encontrar un criador respetable puede no ser tan fácil. Cualquiera que sea la razón por la cual usted desea tener un Golden... ya sea como mascota familiar, como colega en la caza, o para competencias, necesita un perro sano y con buena disposición, un perro que luzca y actúe como el Golden Retriever tradicional. Encontrar un criador de confianza, alguien con experiencia dentro de la raza que críe buenos cachorros, es de suma importancia y puede tomar algún tiempo, pero un buen cachorro vale el esfuerzo.

La búsqueda del binomio cachorro-criador puede ser una experiencia emocionalmente penosa que pondrá a prueba su paciencia y voluntad. Todos los cachorros son adorables y es fácil enamorarse del primero que veamos, pero un Golden

No se decida por un criador que no muestre un innegable amor por la raza.